GARDENING IN THE *Shade*

FROM THE EDITORS OF Horticulture

**HORTICULTURE
BOOKS**

CINCINNATI, OHIO

www.hortmag.com

Gardening in the Shade. Copyright © 2004 by Horticulture Books. Manufactured in China. All rights reserved. No part of this book may be reproduced in any form or by any electronic or mechanical means including information storage and retrieval systems without permission in writing from the publisher, except by a reviewer, who may quote brief passages in a review. Published by Horticulture Books, an imprint of F+W Publications, Inc., 4700 East Galbraith Road, Cincinnati, Ohio, 45236. First edition.

Visit our Web site at www.hortmag.com for information on more resources.

Other fine Horticulture Books are available from your local bookstore or direct from the publisher.

08   07   06   05   04   5   4   3   2   1

Gardening in the shade / from the editors of Horticulture.
    p. cm.
    Includes index.
    ISBN 1-55870-720-4
    1. Gardening in the shade.   2. Shade-tolerant plants.   I. Horticulture.
SB434.7.G27 2004
635.9'543--dc22   2004043335

Edited by Trish Wesley Umbrell, Thomas Fischer, Teri Dunn and Jennifer Ziegler
Design and page makeup by Camillia DeRhodes and Matt DeRhodes
Art direction by Clare Finney
Production coordinated by Sara Dumford and Mark Griffin
Page layout by Camillia DeRhodes
Photography edited by Tina Schwinder
Indexed by Pat Woodruff

photographic ACKNOWLEDGEMENTS

PHOTOGRAPHS

Richard W. Brown: p. 7, p. 12, p. 13, p. 17, p. 46, p. 71

Jonathan Buckley: p. 33 (Design: Maureen Sawyer), p. 103, p. 105, p. 106

David Cavagnaro: p. 49, p.73

Tom Cooper: p. 95

Charles O. Cresson: p. 119

R. Todd Davis: p. 21

John E. Elsley: p. 57 top

Jenks Farmer: p. 106 bottom: left & right

Roger Foley: p. 28, pp. 40-41 (Design: Sally Boasberg), p. 47 (Design: Sally Boasberg)

Garden Picture Library: p. 77 top, Sunniva Harte; p. 99, Neil Holmes; p. 111, John Glover

John Glover: p. 6, pp. 38-39, p. 39 center right, p. 86

Carol Hall: p. 88 left

Pamela J. Harper: p. 10, p. 20 top, p. 112, p. 113

Jerry Harpur: p. 31 top

Lynne Harrison: p. 14 top right, p. 26 top: left & right, p. 55, p. 58 left, p. 66 center & bottom, p. 92 left

Chuck Hassett: p. 94 top left & bottom right

Saxon Holt: p. 23 (Design: Bob Clark), p. 27 (Design: Bob Clark), p. 66 top, pp. 78-83

Lamontagne: p. 94 top right

Andrew Lawson: Cover: top left, p. 24, p. 29, p. 56, p. 57 bottom, p. 67, p. 68, p. 77 bottom, p. 100

Lightworks: p. 97, p. 98

Janet Loughrey: p. 75

New England Wild Flower Society: p. 14 top left, D. Love; center left, NEWFS; center right, D. S. Long; bottom left, F. Bramley; bottom right, D. S. Long; p. 15, D. S. Long; p. 16, Walt/ Louieann Pierowicz

Jerry Pavia: p. 94 bottom center

Photos Horticultural: Cover: top right, p. 26 bottom, p. 44, p. 62, p. 70, p. 101

Positive Images: Cover: bottom, Margaret Hensel; p. 11, Pam Spaulding; p. 18 bottom, Albert Squil lace; p. 22, Margaret Hensel; p. 39 bottom left, Ben Phillips; p. 108 top, Pam Spaulding

Peter Ray: p. 92 right

Susan A. Roth: p. 30, p. 31 bottom (Design: Conni Cross), pp. 34-35, pp. 36-37, p. 39 top left, pp. 42-43 (Stahl Garden), p. 88 right, p. 89, p. 109 bottom, p. 110

Richard Shiell: p. 91

Aleksandra Szwala: p. 25

Michael S. Thompson: p. 8, p. 18 top, p. 19, p. 20 bottom, p. 39 top right & center left, p. 53, p. 58 right, p. 63, p. 64, p. 65, p. 72, p. 94 top center & bottom left, p. 102

James W. Waddick: p. 107, p. 109 top

White Flower Farm: p. 69

ILLUSTRATIONS

Raymond Booth/Fine Arts Society, London; from Japonica Magnifica by Don Elick & Raymond Booth: p. 51, p. 52

Jean Emmons: p. 121

John Matyas: p. 61

Elayne Sears: pp. 123-135

Pamela Stagg: p. 114, p. 115, p. 117

TABLE *of* CONTENTS

introduction

THE PLEASURES AND CHALLENGES OF SHADE GARDENING

Welcome to our book on shade gardening, with a broad range of articles from our recent archives. For every new gardener or homeowner who has cast a daunted or worried eye over the shady portions of his or her yard, for every gardener who has enjoyed success with plants in full sun but not necessarily in shade, this book is for you.

True, shade is frequently considered difficult or a detriment. Limited light and thin or root-infested soil are seen as liabilities. Transforming such spots into attractive gardens seems like a big challenge.

As we thumbed through recent back issues of *Horticulture* magazine, seeking to compile information, advice, and inspiration on the challenging topic of shade gardening for you, we found plenty of interesting articles. More significant, however, is the fact that we were struck again and again by the sense that – actually – there is no problem here! Our authors never paused to wring their hands over the shade that is their lot. Instead, we found them delivering everything from sensible advice to mouthwatering ideas.

And so this is where we invite you to begin your shade-gardening adventures. Rather than lamenting or turning away, jump into this wondrous new world with optimism. Swoon over Ann Lovejoy's tantalizing descriptions of perennials that prosper in dry shade or Joan Means's report on woodland beauties from Asia, follow Gordon Hayward's fascinating instructions on how to fashion a beautiful path through a wooded area on your property, and try Heather McCargo's simple instructions for raising a crop of choice, shade-loving wildflowers from seed. Open this book, open your mind, and allow yourself to get excited about the scenes you will create. You can, and you will!

—Teri Dunn

chapter one
GENERAL TECHNIQUES

TAKING TO THE WOODS

a resourceful gardener sets out to plant beneath big trees

by JOAN MEANS

Regrettably, when we bought our house I was so relieved that we'd found an affordable place that I scarcely looked at the long, narrow plot of land that lay behind it.

The first mortgage payment coincided with the first snowfall; drifts made sparkling billows in the little grove of trees occupying the southwest corner of our acre. "How lovely!" I thought with all the euphoria of the new landowner. I began studying those glossy books that, although they don't exactly explain how a woodland garden is made, tantalize us with photographs of trilliums growing beside a mossy stump. Then spring came, and with the thaw a different page was spread before me. Our patch of woods wasn't just dull, it was an unmitigated mess. Even a horticultural innocent could see that making a garden in these woods would involve more than a sharp eye for aesthetics.

Straddling the property lines of four subdivision plots, the tangled stand of brush and mature trees was typical of eastern Massachusetts, where people have been farming — and abandoning their farms — for centuries. On our side of the line, a dozen tall white pines and an oak served as shelter for poison ivy and Japanese bittersweet; a contorted gray birch was impaled, 3' above the ground, by the iron rim of an old wagon wheel.

Getting Started

"You really need some wildflowers here," my sister-in-law Anne said with a disapproving glance at the northern edge of the woods, where a then lawn petered out under a thick layer of pine needles and hardhack. By then, the second summer in our home, I'd developed a mental block about the nasty details, except when I applauded my husband for pulling out the poison ivy. Someday, we thought, we'd get around to doing more — I had an inchoate vision of pretty little wildflowers making drifts around the feet of rhododendrons. But what gardener can turn down free plants? Before I realized the deeper import of it all, I had accepted offerings from Anne's garden: Canadian ginger (*Asarum canadense*), blue-flowered *Pulmonaria angustifolia*, Dutchman's breeches (*Dicentra cucullaria*), *Iris cristata* 'Alba', and ground-covering European geranium with pink flowers (*Geranium macrorrhizum* 'Ingwersen's Variety'). She even added some divisions of hosta "for a little contrast and structure."

With these ordinary plants, I was launched on a horticulture odyssey that eventually would educate me about how a woodland community works from the bottom up. As a concept, woodland gardening has been around since 1870, when, in his book *The Wild Garden*, the English iconoclast William Robinson suggested that wildflowers be naturalized "in copses, groves, and along woodland walks." Since then, a great many woodland gardens have been created on both sides of the Atlantic, yet it's still curiously difficult to discover how to actually get plants into the ground under the trees. "Humusy soil," "deep preparation," and "not too much shade" is about the extent of the advice, and certainly that's all the guidance I could find when I started digging the ground for Anne's plants.

Rhododendron 'Ken Janek'

For a while, that was enough. I was working in an arc 10' from the closest trees, and —— except for running into some old, woody roots more than a foot in diameter — the process was rather like making any new border. Digging down as far as possible (about 9"), I pulled out rocks and small roots, then forked in about 4" of peat moss and well-rotted cow manure. (Those were the days when our town still had dairy farms; today I must rely on composted leaves.) Despite the big roots, which I left intact, I was able to place most of my plants within 1' of where I wanted them. With a few rhododendrons included for height, the effect was so charming that I resolved to push through to the other side of the trees. Colored and variegated hostas would remain beside the crisply edged lawn to become part of a shade border; the rest of the woods would be devoted to wilder things.

At first, the work was straightforward. We cut down the weedy birches, grubbed out the brush, and removed some of the low branches to let in more sunlight. When we finished, we had a dozen tall trees spaced in a rough triangle measuring 145' along its longest, western edge and about 50' beside the lawn to the north. The only understory tree left was a pagoda dogwood (*Cornus alternifolia*), which, if not showy, has attractive tiered branches. With some pride, I loaded a garden cart with a digging fork, a bag of peat, and four young plants of Cornelian cherry (*Cornus mas*) that I had raised from seed to replace the weed trees. Cornelian cherry is a Eurasian dogwood valued for its pale yellow flowers that appear in early spring, even before forsythia. The leaves have no autumn interest, and the branches splay in all directions like a schizoid shrub, but this 25' tree flourishes in a minimum of direct sunlight. As a bonus, the September crop of olive-shaped fruits, colored like 'Bing' cherries, make a marvelous and unusual jelly when cooked with a touch of lemon.

To my shock, I was scarcely able to shoehorn those seedling trees into the rubbish, stones and interlaced tree roots that lay beneath the pine needles. In a nutshell, I had misjudged the effect of scale. In gardens covering an acre or more of woodland, the dappled sunlight demanded by most flowering plants is achieved by removing entire trees to create a series of open bays and glades connected by a winding path. We couldn't afford to sacrifice any trees in our scaled-down woods, nor did we need to. At some time during the day, nearly all the ground was touched by sunlight slanting between the tree trunks. What we lacked was space. After I'd lined up logs to create paths wide enough to accommodate a garden cart, the only room left for plants was relatively close to the tree trunks in the heaviest root zone.

Gardeners tend to focus on how various degrees of shade may limit plant choice, but clearly all bets are off if you can't provide suitable soil. "I remove all the shallow-rooted trees like maples," a local landscape contractor told me. "Then I use a tiller to cut the roots to a depth of about 9"." This approach may seem brutal, but it's the way William Robinson planted a great sweep of primroses in a birch grove, and it's the way shady borders of any sophistication must be made. Plants like rodgersias, aconites, thalictrums, and many primroses grow in nature where woodlands encroach on fields, and they demand deep, fertile soil. The arboreal response to root surgery varies (conifers are often quite tolerant, while magnolias may die if their roots are merely bruised), but no mature tree can stand having more than a third of its roots removed. Brute force should therefore be used with caution, and then only at the edge of a lawn or glade, or in a parklike grove of widely spaced trees.

In denser stands like our pocket woods, less draconian measures were called for. One possibility was the "take-it-or-leave-it" approach espoused by some American gardeners who, anxious to recapture the native biodiversity now lost in their backyards, introduce only indigenous plants grown in virtually unaltered earth. Ecological correctness works in naturally rich woodlands, but, gardeners being gardeners, most of us yearn to grow blue Himalayan poppies (*Meconopsis betonicifolia*) and black-and-white Japanese jack-in-the-pulpits (*Arisaema sikokianum*). Nor are all forests alike. Eastern New England, for example, has a highly acid, sandy soil that supports a limited native flora. Diversity in my oak-pine woods would be highly unnatural, so even if I limited my garden to American plants such as trilliums and phloxes, I had to find some way to prepare beds of welcoming soil for what were, in reality, alien plants.

When you dig down, you build up. But wouldn't raising the soil level kill the trees? With great trepidation, I filled log-bordered beds with layers of leaves (all kinds, collected from curbsides in suburban towns), peat moss, and garden debris. I was careful not to cover the bark at the base of each tree, so in some places I was able to pack in only a few inches of incipient humus. In others, where the soil had eroded away from a tree, the log walls were more than 1' high. Within a year, the organic material had settled, partly decomposed, and — after topping up — was ready (I was impatient) for the first plants to be inserted into pockets of well-rotted compost. As for the trees, they haven't minded at all.

This was because I made relatively narrow beds that covered small sections of the roots, and filled them with very porous material, as Dr. Gary Watson of the Morton Arboretum, in Lisle, Illinois, explained to me. "Look at it this way," said Watson. "Roots can grow under even an asphalt sidewalk because enough oxygen diffuses into the soil from the sides. If you'd made your beds as broad as a driveway and filled them with heavy loam or clay, it's quite possible that not enough oxygen would have reached the roots.

"Oxygen," Watson emphasizes, "is absolutely vital to the health of the entire length of root. If you'd covered the floor of your woods with only 1" of Midwestern clay your trees would probably be dead. Even too much of the wrong kind of organic mulch can be fatal. Experiments show that 18" of wood chips can be tolerated, but a much thinner layer of grass clippings may kill a tree."

Ranunculus ficaria 'Coppernob' tucks neatly under *Acorus gramineus* 'Ogon'.

Tree Roots

Mental habits die hard. As schoolchildren, many of us were taught that a tree's roots are a mirror image of its top. Today scientists tell us that, except for a few rather inert anchoring roots, the underground life of trees goes on in the oxygen-rich top foot of soil, which is also where water, usable mineral food, and the digestive aid of mycorrhizal fungi are concentrated. Just the same, we all speak of "shallow-rooted" trees like oaks. "For all practical purposes, there are no deep-rooted trees," says Watson. It's nearly impossible to push a trowel into a maple's thick mat of roots, while open places can be found among an oak's sparser spread, but both trees in fact occupy the same level of soil.

Surprisingly, tree roots are much longer than was once estimated — on average, twice the span of the branches, according to Watson. As a result, probably all of us have unwittingly damaged roots, if only by compacting the soil. Happily, most healthy trees eventually make up the deficit. Watson points out that up to 90 percent of a field-grown sapling's roots may be lost when it is transplanted, but, with good timing and intensive care, it grows replacements. Even with mature trees, amputation of a bothersome old root may not be a permanent solution — the surgery simply tickles growth hormones into producing a rash of new young roots,

an underground version of the watersprouts common in apple trees that have been pruned too hard. Moreover, roots are perfectly able to grown up and over plastic or concrete barriers. Sometimes it pays to let sleeping dogs lie. Whenever I want to divide hostas in the bed that I laboriously spaded beside the lawn, I must first drag out bushels of tree roots. By contrast, the raised beds that bridge woody sections of old tree roots have remained free from invasion for decades.

A Shade Garden Matures

But as time passed, other problems developed in the raised beds. The log "walls," by then beautifully covered with moss, had to be replaced with stones: rodents, searching for insects along the rotting inner surfaces, were leaving too many precious wildflowers hanging to dry in the tunnels. More troubling was that many plants began to sicken. I'd thought that deep layers of pure organic material would improve on nature's forest floor, but as the leaves broke down into fragments, the air spaces disappeared, and my beds were no better than a compost pile that needs turning.

"What's the answer?" I asked Ed Leimseider. I'd greatly admired Ed's Connecticut garden, which is devoted to woodland plants of America and Asia. "Dig in plenty of sharp sand," Ed advised, "not the powdery stuff, but almost like fine gravel, so that it makes up about a fourth of the mix." His prescription worked; my plants perked up. What's more, those many grains of sand seem to hold more water by surface tension than is absorbed by humus and peat alone. Now even adamant moisture lovers, like the glorious fall-blooming gentians of the Himalayas, deign to bloom in my garden, and less fussy residents — *Phlox divaricata,* our native American with lavender flowers; *Anemone nemorosa,* the charming little European woodlander; and *Glaucidium palmatum,* a rare Japanese plant with purple, poppylike flowers — are enthusiastically seeding around.

Why should such a broad range of plants suddenly become happy campers? Scientists categorize woodland soils according to how well organic material rots and mixes with the underlying mineral particles. Where rainfall is plentiful and the soil is neither too alkaline nor too acid, bacteria quickly get to work on fallen leaves and earthworms disperse the humus among the mineral particles. The result, much like compost made with loam, is typical of deciduous forests where most woodland species grow — plants like *Trillium grandiflorum* and *Anemone nemorosa.*

By contrast, neither soil bacteria nor earthworms live in dry or very acidic soil, so decomposition is a slow process left mostly to fungi, and only the lowest levels of organic litter turn into humus. Originally, the gravel soil in my woods was covered by only a thin skin of humus lying directly beneath the pine needles, and until I became a human earthworm and added aerating sand, the soil in the new raised beds was deeper but not better. The only plants that really flourished were shallow-rooted acid-lovers like partridge-berry (*Mitchella repens*), bunchberry (*Cornus canadensis*), *Linnaea borealis,* and the stoloniferous Japanese primrose *Primula kisoana.* And, of course, members of the heath family. The heaths — which include heathers, cranberries, blueberries, mountain laurel, and rhododendrons — can be found growing even in the worst-case scenario, where organic material hardly rots at all: on mountaintops, the arctic tundra and sphagnum bogs. Some Malaysian rhododendrons are even epiphytic, joining orchids in the scant organic debris found in the crotches of trees.

Our woods are far from the tropics, but just the same, it's a jungle out there. By altering the soil, I've changed the balance of nature and created a fecund environment in which hundreds of wildflower species from the world's temperate-zone forests happily jockey for space.

In short, I've made a garden, and even apparently artless drifts of plants demand constant editing. The days are gone when I could relax on the back deck and watch poison ivy grow: now I must get out there and dig precious *Hepatica nobilis* seedlings from

L. squamigera in a garden setting

mats of Himalayan maidenhair fern (*Adiantum venustum*), weed the numerous progeny of celandine poppy (*Stylophorum diphyllum*) from a group of hellebores, and move a slow-growing patch of our native American *Shortia galacifolia* out of the reach of the romping stolons of *Primula kisoana.* Under even an ordinary stand of trees, there's more going on than meets the eye, and changing just part of the equation may have unforeseen consequences in a gardener's life.

WITHIN THE WOODLAND
the art and science of growing wildflowers in the shade

by WILLIAM CULLINA

Over half of North America would be covered by some kind of forest if left to its own devices, but not all forests offer the same growing conditions for gardening.

Deciduous trees like maples, ashes, tulip trees and many oaks allow much of the sun's energy to pass through to the ground during winter and early spring, and the wildflowers in these forests respond with a frenetic burst of activity before the trees leaf out. Evergreens — mostly conifers like spruce, pine and fir, which dominate forests in much of Canada, the mountainous and maritime West and some of the South — are another matter. Since these trees do not lose their leaves in winter, the pace of life in the herbaceous layer is more subdued in spring. Many of the wildflowers, such as bunchberry, are evergreen as well, and most are adapted to the cool, acid soils that form under needle-bearing trees. It is important to take into account the type of trees you have while planning your garden. If maples, ashes, basswoods, tulip trees and beeches predominate, incorporate spring ephemerals that do much of their growth and bloom in early spring. If your trees are mainly evergreen, choose wildflowers that are adapted to cool, acid soils and a slower pace of life. If oaks and hickories form your canopy, a mix of the two should work well.

Even so, remember that even a single tree takes up an enormous amount of space, light and water, and that its roots can spread out 50' or more in all directions. Gardening in these conditions can only be done on the tree's terms. A successful woodland garden must be responsive to the needs and rhythms of the trees, but provide just enough light, good soil and water for the wildflowers to thrive.

Letting in Light

Although shade is a given in woodland gardening, it is a difficult thing to quantify. While sun is sun, shade can be anything from the light shadow of a veil to the darkness of a closet. When planning a woodland garden, I like to aim for dappled shade, where the canopy is thin enough to allow sparkles of sunlight to dance across the forest floor. Limb your trees up as high as you can with a pole pruner, or if an arborist is available remove the lower half of the branches that line the trunk. If your woods are dense with young trees or thick conifers, thin out a quarter of the weakest trees to leave gaps in the canopy. (You should have to squint when looking up on a sunny day.) Understory trees and shrubs add depth to the woodland garden, but use them sparingly — not much can grow underneath the double-layered shade of the woody understory. These larger plants are best grouped or scattered lightly through the woods with gaps for herbaceous plants.

Building Good Soil

Woodland soils grow up, not down. The slow deposition of leaves and wood adds organic matter that fuels decomposition, recycles nutrients and builds up topsoil. The topsoil in many forests (with the exception of those where water has deposited sediments in the past) is fairly shallow, and tree roots do their best to occupy every inch of it. In order to provide space for wildflowers, you will likely have to build the soil up. Quite simply, the deeper your topsoil, the better will be both the quality and quantity of wildflowers. The easiest way to do this is to apply a yearly layer of organic mulch such as shredded leaves, bark or aged wood chips — either in the fall or early spring. Adding a few inches of this material (beyond what the trees would supply naturally) will tip the balance, building up in a few years what would otherwise take decades. Layers of decomposing material have the further benefit of feeding beneficial fungi and providing perfect seedbeds for slow-to-germinate plants like trilliums and orchids.

In general, woodland plants are not heavy feeders, and once the soil is healthy enough, no additional fertilizer is necessary. Until that point is reached, however, a light dressing of a balanced organic fertilizer will help immensely. Apply the fertilizer in spring just as the understory begins to emerge — that way, smaller plants can take up what they need before the trees become active.

Providing Water

Fifty years ago, water restrictions and concerns about pollution were pretty much nonexistent. Today, however, we're much more conscious of what spills out of the hose. When we design new gardens, it makes sense to match the plants to the site, selecting plants that can handle summer drought when necessary. Fortunately, many woodland wild-

flowers are active mainly in the spring, so summer dry spells and even an occasional drought will not kill them.

The Different Kinds of Woodland Plants

Woodland gardens put forth a feverish burst of energy in spring. By the summer solstice, though, the garden has transformed into a thousand shades of green, where texture replaces color as the dominant element of design. When planting a woodland garden, therefore, try to follow this rhythm. Plan for and celebrate the early burst of color that evolves gradually into a predominately textural garden in summer — a place of calm, cool shelter from the heat, punctuated by occasional bloom.

Many of the most colorful woodland wildflowers are spring ephemerals, plants that make their aboveground growth early and then retreat underground as the tree canopy fills out and the temperature climbs. Ephemerals provide a quick burst of color when we need it most and require no upkeep in the summer, but they leave gaping holes if used to excess. The most successful woodland gardens use these early players as the first act, relying on longer-lasting wildflowers, ferns and woody plants to fill in after they have left the stage. I call this cohabitational planting, and it is a technique that mirrors closely what happens naturally on the forest floor. Aim for a mix of ephemerals for early-season drama, some specimens like trilliums and orchids for a mid-season epiphany and enduring structural plants such as ferns that will provide interest into the fall.

All the plants mentioned below have been reliably hardy for us in USDA Zone 5, and most are hardy well into Zones 3 and 4. I have tried to pick plants that will perform well over most of the forested parts of the United States and southern Canada.

Ephemerals

The yellow trout lily (*Erythronium americanum*) was a familiar sight in forests near my home growing up, with its ground-hugging leaves mottled in gray and brown like the side

Previous page: When planting a woodland garden, the most satisfying results come from using a combination of early-blooming ephemerals; mid-season specimen plants such as trilliums and orchids; and ferns, groundcover plants, and shrubs for long-term interest. **Left:** clockwise from upper left: Red trillium (*T. erectum*); bunchberry (*Cornus canadensis*); double bloodroot (*Sanguinaria canadensis* f. *multiplex*); celandine poppy (*Stylophorum diphyllum*) and creeping phlox (*P. stolonifera*); *Hepatica americana*; Dutchman's breeches (*Dicentra cucullaria*).

of a brook trout. This species can be frustrating in the garden, producing mats of leaves but very few flowers. A bit of fertilizer in the spring (try one formulated for bulbs) and a bright spot will encourage heavier bloom. The western mountains are blessed with a number of larger species that have freely hybridized in cultivation, producing some outstanding garden plants. *Erythronium* 'Pagoda' is a readily available and very satisfying plant that, under good conditions, will form temporary clumps of 8" to 12" glossy leaves and flaring 2" flowers spaced elegantly on tall stems. Another hybrid, 'White Beauty', is smaller, with creamy white trumpets that flair and curl back at the tips. All the trout lilies are excellent ephemeral companions, quickly retiring underground as the trees leaf out.

As the trout lilies are coming into bloom, Dutchman's breeches (*Dicentra cucullaria*) unfurl filigreed foliage that carpets the ground temporarily in soft blue green, punctuated by arching 6" stems of white flowers that look like upside-down pantaloons. The flowers are effective for about two weeks if the weather remains cool, by which time its close cousin, squirrel corn (*D. canadensis*) takes the stage. Both species spread quickly by seed and cormlets, which can be dug and scattered about after the plants go dormant (just be sure not to disturb them after Labor Day, since they begin to form new shoots for next season that can be easily damaged).

Woodland Stars

The carpeting spring ephemerals pave the way for the stars of the spring woodland. Many of these, including trilliums, bloodroot, lady's slippers and phlox, are not truly ephemeral because their foliage persists well into summer and fall, but spring is certainly their finest hour. By the time the dog days of summer arrive, they are looking a bit tattered and sleepy, and so I like to think of them as vernal exclamations, accents that don't need to hold their place all season. Two of the first to bloom, often when frosts still trace your windshield, are bloodroot (*Sanguinaria canadensis*) and hepatica (both *H. acutiloba* and *H. americana*). Bloodroot lofts blink-and-you'll-miss-them flowers of radiant white that spring from the unrolling leaves. Its bold foliage is quite attractive for most of the summer, especially if moisture falls regularly. Hepaticas are one of my favorite spring wildflowers — little mounds

Iris cristata

of many-petaled violet, blue or white flowers. However, after a wet summer, the usually evergreen foliage becomes tattered and disfigured by the black spot fungi that plague many in the buttercup family. Place hepaticas in a spot with good air movement and drainage and they really shine.

Virginia bluebells (*Mertensia virginica*) emerge from the ground as leafy rosettes stained a deep purple that unfold rapidly and flower

woodland wildflowers
THAT CAN TOLERATE MODERATELY DRY SOIL

Anemonella thalictroides (rue anemone)

Aquilegia canadensis (Canada columbine)

Asarum virginicum (Virginia wild ginger)

Chrysogonum virginianum (golden star)

Gaultheria procumbens (wintergreen)

Geranium maculatum (wild geranium)

Hepatica americana (round-lobed hepatica)

Iris cristata (crested iris)

Mertensia virginica (Virginia bluebells)

Podophyllum peltatum (mayapple)

Sanguinaria canadensis (bloodroot)

Smilacina racemosa (false Solomon's seal)

for about four weeks with ethereal bells of sky blue (or rarely white or rose). They mix beautifully with the buttercup-yellow, four-petalled celandine poppy (*Stylophorum diphyllum*) — an equal match in size and vigor. Both species will liberally self-seed if not deadheaded and may eventually crowd out smaller companions.

As these flowers fade from view, the first of the trilliums begin to bloom. Every spring I am bewitched once again by these elegant wildflowers. I have grown many of the species, but here I will focus on the most satisfactory and easy. Showy trillium (*T. grandiflorum*) is the queen of the genus, with full, white flowers up to 3" across that truly light up the woodland. It is a vigorous species that, once settled in, can form sizable clumps, and if you can think in terms of decades, will seed itself around as well. Its counterpart in the Pacific Northwest is *T. ovatum,* with somewhat smaller white flowers. Red trillium (*T. erectum*), with its faintly fetid, burgundy flowers, is equally easy. Catesby's trillium (*T. catesbyi*) is a good choice for heavy clays in the South. There is a large group of trilliums whose sessile (stemless) flowers nestle in a whorl of typically mottled leaves. The foliar patterns of gray, silver, green and burgundy are at least as interesting as the long-lasting flowers, and I wonder if this camouflage evolved to help hide the plants from color-blind but ravenous deer. Three of the easiest and most readily available are whippoorwill (*T. cuneatum*), with burgundy flowers, yellow trillium (*T. luteum*), with lemon-scented blooms and *T. chloropetalum* and its varieties, with flowers in a range of reds and white.

If you choose carefully, it's possible to have a succession of colorful woodland phloxes in bloom for almost two months. Wood phlox (*P. divaricata*) seeds its way agreeably around the trilliums, providing drifts of blue for several weeks as the trilliums reach their peak. Creeping phlox (*P. stolonifera*) follows on the heels of wood phlox, and its evergreen leaves make a passable ground-hugging carpet for the rest of the year. Ozark phlox (*P. pilosa* subsp. *ozarkiana*) is next to bloom, sporting lavender pinwheels on taller stems. Finally, Alabama phlox (*P. pulchra*) rounds out the display,

Cypripedium parviflora var. pubescens

flowering for us well into June. This species prefers a brighter spot on the edge of the woods.

Lady's slipper orchids remain rarities in gardens, mainly because of the high costs involved in their protracted propagation, but advances in laboratory seedling production should make them cheaper and more readily available over the next few years. Nevertheless, they will continue to have an otherworldly aura about them — they seem almost too intricate and complex to be of this time and place. I have tried most of the native species with degrees of success, but the least demanding are the large and small yellow lady's slippers (*Cypripedium parviflorum* var. *pubescens* and *C. parviflorum*) and the spectacular Kentucky lady's slipper (*C. kentuckiense*). They are closely related plants, sending up stems of alternating, pleated leaves, each tipped with a flower or two in spring. These three species bloom sequentially, so you can have orchids in bloom for a solid month in spring.

stopping WILD COLLECTORS

Commercial wild collecting of woodland wildflowers continues to be a serious threat to their long-term survival. When buying wildflowers, especially slow-growing woodlanders like bloodroot, hepaticas, trilliums and lady's slippers *(Cypripedium pubescens)*, be suspicious of suppliers that sell inexpensive (less than $5 to $10 each) and/or bareroot plants. If you're in doubt, ask the nursery about the source of the plants and buy them only if you're convinced they're nursery-propagated. Your local native plant society is often a good source for lists of reputable vendors.

Large yellow lady's slipper is the first to open, gracing our gardens for Mother's Day every year. By the end of May its blooms are fading and the smaller but more intensely colored small yellow lady's slipper is reaching its peak. It has a chrome-yellow pouch as big as a quail's egg and chocolate petals, and blooms appear in spikes of two or three, unlike the typically solitary flowers of its larger relative. Around the second week in June, the magnificent Kentucky lady's slipper begins to bloom. Its flowers are the largest in the genus, with a moonlight-yellow pouch as big as a hen's egg and chocolate petals suffused with raspberry. When people spot it in the garden there is a kind of whispered awe, as though a movie star had just entered the room. As long as you grow the yellow-flowered species in dappled shade and a moist but gritty soil, they should thrive and double or even triple in size within a reasonably short time.

Groundcovers

Groundcovers excel in the shade, filling in gaps around larger plants and often remaining evergreen throughout the winter. Two of the aristocrats among native groundcovers are wandflower (*Galax urceolata*) and its cousin, the rare and lovely Oconee bells (*Shortia galacifolia*). Both are slow to establish but well worth the wait, clothing themselves in lustrous, deep green leaves.

If you want elegance but don't have the conditions or patience for galax or shortia, consider our native Allegheny spurge (*Pachysandra procumbens*). It is a more refined plant than its Japanese relative, with larger, gray-green foliage that turns burgundy as autumn sets in. The change to red reveals silver mottling that was masked by the green, a pleasing foil for the bottlebrush spikes of cinnamon-scented blooms in early spring. As the flowers fade, the clumps erupt with a burst of fresh green leaves to carry them through the next year. Set them in 2' apart and they will form a solid carpet in two to three years.

Gardening beneath the trees has its challenges, but if you learn to work with them, carving out a bit of extra space for wildflowers to thrive, the results can be spectacular. There is really no other type of gardening where so many plants — from the smallest mosses and groundcovers to shrubs and trees — can all inhabit the same small patch of earth.

A spectacular mid-spring display of wood phlox (*P. divaricata*) and the rare double form of showy trillium (*T. grandiflorum* 'Flore Pleno'). This kind of lavishness is possible only when the plants receive sufficient light, moisture and nutrients.

COPING WITH DRY SHADE

the right plants can green up even the most inhospitable corner

by ANN LOVEJOY

Creating a green haven in dry shade ranks among garden-making's greatest challenges. While shade itself is far from a liability, the combination of deep shade and dry, often rooty soil presents even the most skilled gardener with significant difficulties.

Milium effusum 'Aureum'

Ajuga reptans 'Catlin's Giant'

Altering the environment may be our initial response, and indeed, simple changes can dramatically improve growing conditions. A program of soil improvement is essential for providing nourishment for roots in a competitive environment. Judicious thinning of tree branches brings more light to persistently dark places. (When the darkness comes from walls, light-reflective white paint and mirrors will maximize the available light.) It is equally important, of course, to select plants that have proven adaptable to such tough conditions. By altering the growing environment and choosing appropriate plants, the resourceful gardener can achieve exciting results.

To discover what will succeed in your dry, shady garden, look at what grows happily in your local woods. Towering firs, cedars, and madronas intermingled with alders and maples surround my northwestern garden. In the dry shade at the trees' feet grow glossy, evergreen mahonias and leathery salal, evergreen and deciduous huckleberries, rosy currant and bird-sown hollies. Beneath the shrubs' branches runs a host of perennials, from robust coltsfoot, false Solomon's seal, and sword ferns to dainty trilliums and tiny orchids. In New England woods I would find elderberry, witch hazel and dogwoods, dolls' eyes and fox grape, mayapples and wake-robins, while the Deep South offers mountain laurel and azaleas, bowman's root and wild ginger. We can look farther afield as well, choosing woodland plants from all over the temperate world. The English woods provide additional inspiration with their famous bluebells, as do the magnificent mountain woods of eastern Europe and Asia, including the Himalayas.

Whatever their provenance, woodland plants have similar needs. All tolerate or even require shade and compete well for nutrients in crowded settings. Most have low or seasonal water requirements, generally preferring to be wet in winter and spring and dry in summer. Many bloom early or late in the year, when the leaf canopy is thin or nonexistent, and experience most of their active growth in fall, winter (when roots flourish), and early spring, going dormant as summer heats up. Shade gardeners soon discover that, because most woodland wildflowers are early bloomers, it takes some effort to develop an extended flowering season. The solution is to expand the palette of plants to include a variety of evergreen or semi-evergreen shrubs and perennials that will help plantings look furnished at all times.

Shrubs

Small or large evergreen shrubs provide a sturdy backbone for any planting, and many of them tolerate dry shade with aplomb. The false cypress clan (*Chamaecyparis* spp.) offers numerous fine forms, notably selections of western Lawson cypress (*C. lawsoniana*; USDA Zone 5). These come in a great range of sizes (from 6' to 60') and colors, shading from rich greens through icy blues and grays to clear yellow and old gold. They will not tolerate deep and lasting drought, but given decent soil, summer irrigation and light or partial shade, many forms of this western native make fast-growing, handsome trees or shrubs.

Creeping Siberian false cypress (*Microbiota decussata*; Zone 2; 18" high by 6' wide) is a slow-growing conifer that broadens decorously in shade, where its toasty winter color looks warm and chocolaty beside greener companions. This shaggy sprawler appreciates well-drained soils and grows happily in sun or quite deep shade.

Both butcher's broom (*Ruscus aculeatus*; Zone 7; to 4') and the similar-looking Alexandrian laurel (*Danaë racemosa*; Zone 8; to 3') are stiffly upright little evergreens with long, flat leaves and spiky stems decorated in fall and winter with fat red berries. Alexandrian laurel is the more graceful of the two, with the wispy look of bamboo. Indeed, it partners delightfully with heavenly bamboo (*Nandina domestica*; Zone 7; 3'–6'), a feathery little shrub with marvelous fall and winter leaf color, creamy or shell-pink flowers, and small red berries tucked among its slim, tapered leaves. Once established, this lacy-looking confection will compete admirably with tree roots and take dry soils in stride. Alexandrian laurel and nandina both fruit best when grown in small colonies in light or broken shade.

Skimmias also need company because the sexes are on separate plants, and females need a male nearby in order to bear fruit. *Skimmia japonica* (Zone 7; 2'–5') offers a multitude of named forms. All are compact evergreens with leathery, creased foliage. Their rosy buds open into small, fragrant clusters of white flowers that are followed by shiny berries, which may be red, black, or white.

Many daphnes are happiest in shade, and certain of them tolerate summer-dry soils. Laurel spurge (*Daphne laureola*; Zone 7; to 4') seeds itself into woodlands and shaded meadow verges, filling the air with piercingly sweet perfume from late winter into spring. Leggy and modestly good-looking, this evergreen needs firm support from companions such as small rhododendrons or mountain laurels. *Daphne odora* 'Aureomarginata' (Zone 7; 4–8'), with leaves edged in pale gold, is slightly hardier than the plain form and blooms generously in shady sites with dry, open-textured soils.

Though nearly always recommended for sunny spots, certain pyracanthas will grow and flower abundantly in dry shade. In my garden, yellow-berried *Pyracantha* 'Gold Rush' thrives in extremely dry soil, sandwiched between an elderly weeping birch and a lusty holly.

Mountain laurels are notably accepting of seasonally dry soils and shady sites. Standard forms are mannerly, upright shrubs that open clusters of white or pale pink goblet-shaped flowers from baroquely pleated buds. A recent introduction, *Kalmia latifolia* 'Shooting Star' (Zone 4; 4'–6'), has more open, informal white flowers that appear a bit later than usual. New colors include 'Sarah' (to 5'), with rosy blossoms above bronzed new foliage, and 'Bullseye' (to 8'), with a strikingly striped burgundy eye zone.

Dicentra 'Luxuriant'

Polygonatum odoratum 'Variegatum'

Euphorbia amygdaloides var. robbiae

In small spaces dwarf evergreens are invaluable, particularly those with multiple gifts. Dwarf sweet box (*Sarcococca hookeriana* var. *humilis*; Zone 6; to 18") runs quietly between bigger companions, sending up short stems decked with glossy, tapered leaves and, in winter, tufts of whiskery ivory flowers that exude a sumptuous scent of honey and vanilla. *Leucothoe axillaris* (Zone 6; 3'–4') and *L. walteri* (Zone 5; to 4') are southeastern natives with elegantly arching branches and shiny foliage that colors hotly in autumn and winter; new spring growth is a coppery red. Their cascading shape contrasts wonderfully with the stiff fans and splayed seedpods of *Iris foetidissima* (Zone 6; to 2').

Deciduous hydrangeas provide frothy mounds of long-lasting bloom in almost any color you like, from white, cream or ivory through pink, lavender and mauve, to rose, ruby, sky blue and turquoise, all enriched by vinaceous purples. Young plants need supplemental water for a few seasons, but mature specimens are indestructible dowagers of the dry, shady garden. Tree peonies, notably *Paeonia delavayi* (Zone 5; to 4') and *P. lutea* (Zone 5; 6'–8') and their hybrids, also bloom prolifically in light or partial shade, and established plants are not at all disturbed by summer drought. Their splendid foliage remains lovely long after the fleeting flowers have faded.

Perennials

A surprising number of perennials will mingle with these shrubs in dry, shady borders and increase happily. Many hostas and ferns grow well in such conditions, including the majestic partnership of *Hosta* 'Krossa Regal' (Zone 3; to 3'), dapper in blue-gray seersucker and the golden-scaled male fern *Dryopteris affinis* 'The King' (Zone 4; to 4'), which has ornately tassled frond tips.

Wood spurges also enjoy these conditions, sowing themselves into their preferred positions at the base of trees and shrubs. Ruddy-leaved *Euphorbia amygdaloides* 'Rubra' (Zone 5; to 2') performs best when not overcrowded and can be prone to powdery mildew in very dry settings. Robb's spurge (*E. a.* var. *robbiae*; Zone 5; to 3') is a vigorous creeper whose wandering ways are kept nicely in check by dry soils and deep shade, where its lustrous leaves and chartreuse inflorescences are welcome. A thicketing Himalayan, *E. griffithii* (Zone 5; to 4'), grows and flowers well in deep shade, but cultivars such as the hot red 'Fireglow' and the brick-red 'Dixter' color better in partial sun.

Woodland wildflowers such as bleeding hearts and foxgloves make themselves thoroughly at home in dry shade. The vigorous hybrid *Dicentra* 'Luxuriant' (Zone 3; 1') offers slate-blue, lacy foliage

Lamiastrum galeobdolon

and a long succession of warm red flowers. Common *D. spectabilis* (Zone 3; to 3') won't bloom all summer but will hold its leaves far longer in shade than in sun. Tall foxgloves (*Digitalis purpurea*; Zone 4; 3'–6') rise like belled jester's wands, tipped in cream, pink or soft purple. 'Sutton's Giant Apricot' self-sows reliably in peachy patches, provided it is kept well away from the purple wildlings, and so too will the gentle 'Sutton's Primrose'.

All sorts of hardy geraniums work their way into dry shade. Mourning widow (*Geranium phaeum*; Zone 4; to 3') spreads in enormous clumps under a birch tree in my garden. Most of the clumps are variegated like their mother (*G. p.* 'Variegatum'), with dim, purple-black flowers. As the shade lightens, they are joined by blue and white forms of meadow geranium (*G. pratense*; Zone 5; to 4'), long bloomers that repeat well when kept from setting their copious seed. At ground level, *G. macrorrhizum* (Zone 4; 1') in many forms canters across the ground, its large, furry leaves punctuated for much of the summer by pink or rosy flowers.

Where summers are hotter, plants that fade fast in full sun may linger longer in shade, however dry. In North Carolina, garden designer Edith Eddleman grows silver-edged Solomon's seal (*Polygonatum odoratum* var. *pluriiflorum* 'Variegatum'; Zone 4; to 2.5') on a sandy bank under an oak tree, and again smack against the base of a *Magnolia grandiflora*. Many little bulbs flourish in dry shade for her, notably fall-blooming *Crocus goulimyi* (Zone 3; 3") and the marbled *Cyclamen hederifolium* (Zone 5; 5"), both of which demand a dry dormant period in the summer. Bluebells of several kinds and ground orchids, including a number of hybrid bletillas, also persist and bloom well in dry shade.

groundcovers for DRY SHADE

Good groundcovers for these difficult conditions include many of the dead nettles, particularly forms of *Lamium maculatum* (Zone 3; 8"). 'White Nancy', 'Beacon Silver', and 'Cannon's Gold' are all strong performers in dry shade. A close cousin, yellow archangel (*Lamiastrum galeobdolon*; Zone 4; 1'), is a weedy sprawler in its typical form, but the selection 'Hermann's Pride' is a glorious carpeter, with narrow, dark leaves abundantly splashed with metallic silver and bearing masses of soft yellow flowers over a long season. Bugleweeds are also good candidates, notably forms of *Ajuga reptans* (Zone 3; 3"–10"). The darker of these tend to be slow spreaders in dry soils, but given time they pour into luxuriant carpets of burgundy, purple or near black. Spinach ajuga (*A. r.* 'Metallica Crispa') has crinkled, molasses-colored leaves while 'Atropurpurea' is bronzed burgundy. Both bear deep blue flowers. Paler 'Tricolor' is washed with cream and rose and sage while 'Silver Carpet' is fine-textured and suitably pewtery.

Eddleman's extensive collection of ivies does well on the same arid, shady bank, where their curly leaves and wavy margins eddy and flow, suggesting the rippling movement of water. The ivy leaves collect humus over time, and hellebores self-sow in the pockets of richer soil, as does *Arum italicum* (Zone 5; 18") and the native green dragon, *Arisaema dracontium* (Zone 4; 2'). Of the epimediums, she finds that *E. ×versicolor* 'Sulphureum' (Zone 5; to 15") is the best of this shade-loving genus for really dry situations where it is often joined by self-sown blue mistflower (*Eupatorium coelestinum*; Zone 5; 6").

Grasses

Grasses that enjoy dry shade include evergreen, cream-striped *Luzula maxima* 'Marginata' (now known as *L. sylvatica* 'Marginata'; Zone 6; 18"), which quickly builds into large and handsome tussocks, and sea oats (*Chasmanthium latifolium*; Zone 3; 3'–5'). Bowles' golden grass (*Milium effusum* 'Aureum'; Zones 6–9; 18") is a fitful perennial that self-sows abundantly in dry shade where its golden leaves and airy seed heads are turned to gilded aureoles by slanting sun rays.

Epimedium versicolor 'Sulphureum'

soil PREPARATION

Because any dry, relatively dark setting is a challenging one, it makes sense to give those carefully chosen plants the best possible start. This means amending the existing soil, which is often dusty and exhausted. To improve both tilth and drainage, add copious quantities of humus. My own favorite combination is a blend of compost and aged or pit-washed dairy manure. Lay it down thickly, adding generous amounts of chopped or pelletized alfalfa (a common goat food), which causes a synergistic release of nitrogen when combined with manures. If the soil is not desperately poor, you can dig in this mixture before planting. Otherwise, remove the soil to a depth of 1' (or more, if you are young and strong or wealthy enough to pay somebody else to do this part). Replace it with fresh topsoil, not neglecting the amendments outlined above. Heavy, clay-based soils will benefit from the addition of coarse builder's sand (the kind used on roads in winter, not sandbox stuff, which turns clay into adobe) to increase drainage. An annual mulch of compost and aged manure will keep your renewed soil in good heart. This may seem a lot of effort, but the result is worth it all, for your dry, difficult site will be transformed into a living garden that remains attractive all through the year.

chapter two
GENERAL DESIGN

THE MANY SHADES OF SUNLIGHT

how patterns of light and shadow shape a garden

by LUCY HARDIMAN

I begin every day with a walk through the garden. On most days, I sneak out at lunch for another look around; and each day ends as it started, with a twilight tour of the beds and borders. Obsessed, yes; crazy, no.

Each time I venture into the garden I am delighted, humbled and amazed by its changing character. As the sun shifts in the sky depending on the season, as the clouds come and go, the patterns of light and shade vary endlessly, highlighting or obscuring the colors, shapes and textures of the plants.

The quality, intensity and distribution of light determine, in large part, what we grow and where it's planted. Plants that require full sun, six to eight hours a day, to flower or produce fruit are best situated in west- or south-facing exposures. Part sun, often described as four to six hours of sun per day, most often occurs in parts of the garden that are on an east-west axis. Along this axis, the eastern portion basks in the gentle, slanting rays of the morning sun, while the western reaches are subjected to the strong illumination of the sun as it climbs higher in the sky. Although each area experiences a degree of shade, the plant palette for each space should be predicated on the amount and intensity of the available sunlight.

Direct sunlight has(seeing. Gardens that receive no protection or shelter from direct light can appear flat as a pancake, without a (forms and highly textured foliage in such bright light is akin to putting on a pair of 3-D glasses. Immediately, the space reads as three-dimensional, layered and dramatic. Another way to add punch to a sunny border is to incorporate shrubs, perennials and annuals with black-green or purplish-toned foliage for instant contrast. Shiny-leaved foliage will reflect light instead of absorbing it, adding pockets that seem to sparkle. If creating shade is the

object, a judiciously placed tree or several large shrubs will alter the play of light and shade. West- or south-facing terraces, decks or patios can be inhospitable spaces for late-afternoon and evening activities, even without the addition of trees planted in containers.

Shade comes in an array of guises, complete with complicated and confusing explanations. Part shade connotes four to six hours of sunlight that strikes plants in the morning hours and moves on by early afternoon. Plant choices for this particular shade designation are many and manifold. Some sun worshipers tolerate a bit of afternoon shade, while others appreciate a respite from full sun.

Two hours of sun is defined as partial shade and is the desired setting for what we think of as shade plants, such as hostas, epimediums, foxgloves and hellebores.

In filtered-light situations, denizens of the woodland or forest floor receive no direct light, but thrive in the diffused and sheltering light afforded by the overhead canopy of deciduous and broadleaved evergreen trees and shrubs. Deep shade prevails under the overhanging branches of needled evergreens, where virtually no light reaches the ground.

Previous page: Early-morning light has a reddish cast that accentuates hot-colored flowers and foliage. **Above:** Lavenders, blues and whites glow in the ghostly light of dusk.

Overly shady gardens can feel oppressive and overwhelming, especially if trees and large shrubs haven't been pruned and maintained. Removing the lower limbs and lifting the canopy of deciduous trees creates planting pockets at ground level for small shrubs, perennials, bulbs and groundcovers, replicating a natural, layered woodland. Foliage can be used to create the illusion of brightness, electrifying the shade garden. Chartreuse and shades of yellow create pools of light, while leaves variegated with white and cream reflect light, making the surrounding areas appear brighter. Mirrors mounted in old door- or window frames and hung along a fence line or at the end of a sight line increase the illusion of light and spaciousness. Even the archetypally Victorian gazing ball can be artfully placed to reflect its surroundings. A terrace on the north side of a house or structure may receive no direct sun, but it can benefit from light bouncing off the walls. These conditions are perfect for pocket borders or containers filled with shade-tolerant trees, shrubs, annuals, perennials and grasses.

All of the structural elements that make up the framework of a garden — fences, hedges, trees, large shrubs, houses and outbuildings — have a direct effect on the amount of available light in different areas of the garden. Beds and borders immediately adjacent to the north side of a building are shaded and protected by the structure. Tall shrubs, perennials and vegetables can be planted on the north side of a garden without casting shadows on shorter companions placed in front of them.

Concrete foundations, siding, stone walls and walkways absorb light, heating up the garden. Plants sited near west- and south-facing foundations and walls need to be able to withstand reflected heat along with intense light. On the other hand, such sheltered hot spots in the garden are good places to experiment with plants from warmer climates.

As the sun moves through the course of the day, the amount of light that each area of the garden receives changes. A border that began the day in shade may be exposed to full sun from midafternoon until late evening. Conversely, a bed that is in the path of morning rays may be shielded from the heat of the day as the sun heads westward over the top of a house, outbuilding or tree. Careful and considered placement of plants with translucent foliage, such as cannas, smoke trees and grasses, maximizes backlighting, a phenomenon that occurs in periods of low light — early in the morning or just before dusk. The foliage comes alive, shimmering like colored jewels in the dying light.

Sunrise finds the sun at its lowest point in the sky, creating a soft, hazy effect. Early-morning light is even, without the play of shad-

Above: Backlighting brings out new dimensions in plants with translucent foliage.

Right: A mirror creates a magical sense of light and depth in shady sections of the garden.

ow that occurs as the sun rises higher in the sky. The angle at which the sun's rays pass through the earth's atmosphere early in the day diffuses light, causing colors to take on a reddish cast. Colors at the hot end of the spectrum (yellow, red and orange) glow and really stand apart in morning light, while darker, more somber hues appear dull and drab.

At midday, the light of the sun passes directly through the atmosphere, unaffected by the particulate matter and dust that colors morning light. It beams with great intensity on the earth below. From noon to midafternoon, colors that appeared fresh and pristine earlier in the day fade out in the harsh, white light of the full sun. Reds, oranges and bright yellow, the hot colors, glitter and gleam in the searing light and heat of the full sun, while paler pastel shades lose their definition and seem to disappear, leaving the garden pallid and listless.

As the sun sinks lower in the sky and twilight approaches, the light assumes a luminous, reflective presence. Gone is the red-orange tinge of earlier in the day, replaced by a bluish tone. At dusk, the garden assumes a mysterious guise as hard outlines and shapes recede, becoming indistinct and blurry as bright color fades into obscurity. Lavenders, blues and whites become more visible in the fading light. They are the perfect colors for containers and borders on and around places where people congregate in the evening.

As the plants grow and mature, the hard outlines of our gardens become blurry, hidden from view by the trunks, branches, foliage, and flowers of the plants that we so carefully selected and nurtured. Neighboring houses disappear behind the sheltering treetops. Trees

and shrubs that began life as puny sticks suddenly exert their influence, casting shade over their companions and causing us to rethink our choices. Gardens are a living art form, and nature is always reminding us that our job is never done.

The interplay of sunny and shady areas (created by trees as well as different foliage colors) expands the sense of space and enriches the character of the garden.

FINDING INSPIRATION IN NATURE

basic design principles to get you started

by C. Colston Burrell

Many gardeners shy away from garden design, thinking that they lack the skills to come up with their own cohesive plan. Yet what they really lack is confidence, which comes from a basic understanding of the elements of design and the steps to go about making a plan. Whether you're designing a garden under a tree, beside a house or within a woodland, your basic design principles remain the same. By emulating designs found in nature and by paying attention to color, foliage, form and texture, you can have a beautiful and satisfying shade garden.

No matter how large or small your shaded garden is, looking to nature for inspiration can help you get the most out of your efforts. Patterns are common in nature, from shadows cast by dancing leaves to the ridgelines formed by overlapping mountains. There are also more subtle patterns created by the way plants grow and interact with each other. Nature's patterns help us design attractive shade gardens where plants can be expected to thrive.

Think in Layers

Layers add visual as well as ecological complexity to a shade garden. From a design standpoint, mimicking the different levels of the natural forest can help you to define different garden spaces and create atmosphere. In the forest, the canopy, or topmost layer, creates a monumental feeling of space. Below the canopy the understory brings the overhead enclosure down to a more intimate level, like the ceiling of a cozy living room. Shrubs divide the space beneath the understory into garden rooms while screening views and providing enclosure or barriers at the garden's edges. Finally, the ground layer, like the furnishings in a room, introduces the visual complexity and seasonal interest that all keen gardeners crave.

You don't have to garden in a mature forest to use layers in your garden. For example, a large tree in the lawn often makes too much shade to support good turf. Why not transform that spot into a garden? A single flowering tree can create shelter for a bed of shade-loving plants. Likewise, an informal hedge of viburnums or rhododendrons will screen the garden from the neighbors or create a private hideaway.

Play with Color

The colors of flowers and foliage draw us to certain plants. Color preferences are as individual as our fingerprints; what delights you may horrify your neighbors. Color theory, based on the arrangement of complementary or contrasting colors on a color wheel, dictates a few simple guidelines for composing a planting scheme. The most important consideration, however, is staying true to your own tastes.

Different colors create different moods in the garden. Combinations of single colors, called monochromatic color schemes, produce

garden pictures that are cohesive and contemplative. Single-color gardens are perfect for people with strong color preferences. Combinations of cool colors — pinks, blues and purples — are restful and seem to meld into the background. Warm-color gardens of yellows, oranges and reds are like a sultry breeze on a summer

afternoon. They are riveting, sensual and seem to leap forward from the garden to meet your eye.

Complementary colors — those opposite each other on the color wheel — make for exciting combinations. Because they share no pigments, paired opposites like blue and yellow or purple and orange create brilliant contrast. A monotonous combination can be enlivened with a splash of a complementary color. In a blue and purple scheme of phlox and Virginia bluebells (*Mertensia virginica*), for instance, adding a patch of bright yellow daffodils or scarlet fire pinks (*Silene virginica*) will give it some zip. Likewise, in a red, purple and yellow scheme, deep orange will add a bit of zing.

Make the Most of Foliage

Shade combinations are particularly dependent on good foliage, since many bulbs and wildflowers bloom fleetingly in the spring and disappear in summer. Strong forms, along with interesting textures, will give shade gardens season-long interest in spite of a scarcity of flowers. A good rule of thumb when designing combinations is to avoid using more than one plant per combination that has inferior foliage. You can always get away with a bleeding heart going dormant if you have ferns and umbrella plants with great foliage to fill the void it leaves.

Consider Form and Texture

Contrasting shapes and habits, whether prostrate, upright, rounded, spiky or spear-shaped are key to creating a pleasing tapestry of foliage in a shady garden. Flat, ground-hugging plants are particularly important since they fill in gaps at the front of the garden and can enliven the garden's profile by making it appear to undulate, like a wave. When prostrate plants are used to surround plants with contrasting forms, they set them off to great advantage.

Rounded forms are the most common in the garden. They can unify a shaded bed or woodland glade by providing it with continuity. Billowing plants like phlox and Bowman's root (*Gillenia trifoliata*) can be used to link more dramatic plants together. Spiky forms like irises, sedges, tall ferns and burnets (*Sanguisorba* spp.) serve as the exclamation points of the garden, breaking up horizontal lines. Tall, perpendicular flower spikes like bugbanes (*Cimicifuga* spp.) and erect fern fronds add a bit of lift.

Above: Monochromatic color schemes are nearly foolproof, and when skillfully implemented, are both serene and elegant. **Right:** Color contrasts can also be highly effective, as with these yellow tulips and blue *Brunnera macrophylla.*

Colors are classed as primary or secondary based on their purity of hue. The primary colors —
red, blue and yellow — are the hues from which all colors stem. Combining primary colors
creates the secondary colors orange, green and violet.

When you add black to a pure hue you create a shade, and when you add white you get
a tint. Most flowers come in shades and tints rather than in pure hues. Different combinations of shades and tints create varied effects that can leap from the garden like a beacon,
or melt away like a dreamy Monet painting.

Foliage color, whether green, red, yellow or gray, can play a major role in bringing color
to dark, shaded spaces. Yellow and chartreuse-leaved plants — like Bowles' golden sedge
(*Carex elata* 'Aurea'), golden creeping Jenny (*Lysimachia nummularia* 'Aurea') and the gold-
and cream-splashed comfrey, *Symphytum* 'Goldsmith' — brighten the shadows. White and
silver variegated leaves, which reflect light, can also lighten shade.

In this color wheel the pure
hues are in the middle ring;
shades — colors darkened by the addition of black — in the outer ring, while
tints — colors lightened by the addition of
white — are in the inner ring. Unlike simpler ver-
sions of the color wheel, this one includes more subtle
gradations of green, blue and purple — colors especially
prevalent in flowers and foliage.

Texture refers to the visual impression of a plant's tactile qualities. With plants, texture can be fine, medium or coarse. From a distance finely textured foliage appears misty and creates a feeling of depth when contrasted with bolder foliage. Examples of finely textured plants include corydalis, ferns and wild bleeding heart (*Dicentra eximia*). Far more common are the medium-textured plants, the mainstays of the shade garden's fabric, such as wild ginger, epimediums and hellebores. Boldly textured foliage creates drama. It stops the eye even from a distance and snaps any garden picture into focus. Picture a colossal chartreuse hosta, like 'Sum and Substance', or the enormous rounded leaves of umbrella plant (*Darmera peltata*) beside a stream and you will understand its power. By mixing and matching various sizes, shapes, and colors of both flowers and foliage, you will create combinations that are beautiful and exhilarating.

Putting It All Together

Once you understand the building blocks of a good garden, there are many ways to work out a successful garden plan. Some people prefer to start with a drawing, while others can visualize the garden in their mind's eye and lay the garden out directly on-site. An easy way to get a sense of how your garden will look is to create combinations at a nursery by assembling the actual plants. I usually make a list of the plants that I want to grow, and then do a rough sketch of the profile of the garden bed. Designers call this an elevation, and it gives them a sense of how the garden will look once it is planted.

To create a harmonious garden bed, start by choosing a few key colorful combinations that have a balance of forms and contrasting textures. A simple way to think about combinations is to plan them in threes, thinking of the plants as corners forming the angles of a triangle. If a tree trunk serves as your first corner, a spiky accent plant such as a bugbane (*Cimicifuga* spp.) could serve as your second corner while a bold textured plant like a hosta or Japanese yellow bells (*Kirengeshoma palmata*) could become the third corner completing the triangle.

Likewise, if you already have a large mass of shrubs, such as a backdrop of viburnums or witch hazels you could balance and mimic its shape with a shorter drift of a dense, persistent perennial like Japanese yellow bells or a clump of smaller shrubs such as poet's laurel (*Danae racemosa*) or sweetspire (*Itea virginica*). Try to avoid placing the second, smaller mass directly in front of the shrubs so that you start to form another triangle. For the third corner you'll need something dramatic; consider a smaller drift of something like a bold hosta, shredded umbrella plant (*Syneilesis*

spp.) or umbrella leaf (*Diphylleia cymosa*).

Once the first triad is complete, move a short way down the bed and create a second combination, and if space allows, a third and so on. Ultimately you will go back and link these combinations together with complementary forms and textures that will unify the bed. But first, you must flesh out your triads to make interesting compositions for each garden picture. If you have three dramatic corner plants in your triad complement them with rounded forms like 'Firetail' knotweed (*Persicaria amplexicaulis* 'Firetail'), and create some horizontal masses with large drifts of phlox or Solomon's seal (*Polygonatum* spp).

If you used mostly rounded forms add some lift with the vertical forms of Dixie wood fern (*Dryopteris ×australis*), Goldie's fern (*D. goldiana*) or a spiky astilbe like 'Purple Candle'. These vertical forms will break up the strong horizontal lines created by the three masses and make the combination more dramatic. Remember that tree trunks can also serve as strong vertical accents.

Next you need to unify the bed by filling the gaps. To link the series of dramatic pictures you have created, use drifts of persistent foliage, like ferns, sedges or groundcovers. Try some of the smaller ferns like New York fern (*Thelypteris noveboracensis*), maidenhair (*Adiantum* spp.) or holly ferns (*Polystichum* spp.). Masses of Lenten roses (*Helleborus ×hybridus*), large patches of low groundcovers such as wild ginger (*Asarum* spp.) or barrenwort (*Epimedium* spp.) work exceptionally well for unifying a bed. Vary their height so the tapestry of vegetation rises and falls like waves and keeps the garden interesting.

Break up the groundcover plantings from time to time with some drifts of bulbs, or variegated Solomon's seal, to add a little lift. Mix ephemeral bulbs and wildflowers, such as trilliums, European wood anemone (*Anemone nemorosa*) and daffodils with these persistent species.

Finally, think about adding a few tulips for a burst of color. Though they are not perennial in most woodland situations, they are inexpensive and sure to perk up a spring combination.

Bold clumps of cinnamon fern (*Osmunda cinnamomea*) and goatsbeard (*Aruncus dioicus*) form a roughly triangular outline that provides the structure for this planting, while the bold, rounded leaves of hostas act as a textural counterpoint. Groundcovers such as epimediums and European ginger (*Asarum europaeum*) complete the picture. Using this triangle-based technique makes it much easier to design eye-pleasing combinations of shade plants.

This superb composition achieves its effect by creating horizontal layers of contrasting texture and scale. The chief ingredients are *Viburnum plicatum* f. *tomentosum* 'Shasta' (the layered shrub at top), a white-flowered cultivar of *Phlox stolonifera*, a groundcover, cascading, golden-leaved *Hakonechloa macra* 'Aureola' and low-growing azaleas and European ginger (*Asarum europaeum*).

Left: Climbing hydrangea (*Hydrangea anomala* subsp. *petiolaris,* Zones 4–8). **Above, left to right:** 'Buttercup' English ivy (*Hedera helix* 'Buttercup', Zones 6–9); *Dicentra scandens* (Zones 7–10); *Clematis macropetala* (Zones 3–9); *Lonicera* ×*tellmanniana* (Zones 5–9); star jasmine (*Trachelospermum jasminoides,* Zones 8–10).

Go with the Flow

In nature, change is the rule. Since you cannot freeze any single moment you must learn to celebrate nature's dynamic flux. Plants will increase in size. Some will die. Others will self-sow and change the look of the beds. This evolution helps to give the garden a settled, mature look.

The controlling hand of the gardener will be necessary to guide this evolution, however. Some plants will end up in the wrong spot. Vigorous spreaders will start to displace choice plants. Dead plants will leave gaps that must be filled. In the end, gardening is a partnership with nature. As the garden evolves, your ideas will evolve with it. With the help of nature, your silent partner, a shaded garden increases in beauty and complexity with each passing year. And you can take all the credit.

what you need to know about

TREE ROOTS

Many gardeners believe that a tree's root system forms a tight, deep sphere belowground — essentially a mirror image of its branches. Recent research has shown, however, that most trees do not have a tap root and that their root systems form a wide, shallow disk that can extend twice as far as the tree's crown. Moreover, 80 percent of the feeder roots are in the upper 6"–8" of soil. These facts have significant repercussions for gardening practices. First, gardeners should try to protect the root systems of important trees as far as possible. This means keeping major soil disturbances at least 15' from the trunk. Be cautious if you're regrading the soil near a tree — adding only a few inches of soil on top of a tree's root zone can cause slow, irreversible decline. If you want to plant shrubs or perennials near an established tree, do so with hand tools. Finally, an area of mulch around the trunk is much better for the tree than lawn, which competes for moisture and nutrients.

The materials you use to create a woodland path deserve careful thought. For example, this is one of the few environments in which wood chips don't look out of place. Pine needles or shredded leaves or bark would also be appropriate and visually appealing. Avoid materials with a formal appearance, such as brick or dressed stone.

When you're laying out a woodland path, keep in mind that gentle curves are more intriguing than straight lines. The curves in this path, for example, lead the eye into the distance, where a welcoming bench can just be glimpsed. If the bench were in plain sight, the pleasure of discovery would be ruined.

A WAY THROUGH THE WOODS

thoughts on designing a sylvan path

by GORDON HAYWARD

A woodland path, whether it leads through a small copse of trees or through acres of forest, has the power to create a mood that is unlike any other in the garden. While flowered borders in full sun stimulate the eye with bright colors, a woodland path is relaxed and subdued.

foliage creating an interplay of greens and textures. In autumn brilliant red, orange and yellow leaves hold overhead for a week or two and then fall to the ground. And in winter the woodland path leads walkers or cross-country skiers past evergreens and among gray-and-black tree trunks.

You don't need to own acres of woodland in order to create and enjoy a woodland path. My wife and I cleared one through a small copse on our property. We planted flowering shrubs to enclose the woods and ran the path between plantings of perennials, ferns, and smaller shrubs. Another good place for a path is through a narrow band of woods that separates one building or garden space from another. And a path need not be heavily planted. You could simply clear a path through a small woodland that leads past existing landmarks, such as unusual trees or shrubs, clearings,

Where a lawn is sunny and open, a woodland path is shaded and enclosed. Such a path is a private area that offers a cool and contemplative respite.

A woodland path also offers the potential for remarkable scenic variety. It can lead you to a mossy boulder that is a natural garden in itself, then on to an expansive view of distant hills. One moment you might be in full shade, the next in a pool of light. A path offers seasonal changes as well. In spring azaleas, rhododendrons, and any number of shade-tolerant perennials planted along the path will add drama and color. In summer the path is shaded and cool, with

streams or views. Whatever the approach, a woodland path leads to an increased appreciation of the beauty and peace inherent in a woodland.

Three paths that I have played a role in creating provide examples of the variety possible. The smallest is the one on our property in southern Vermont (USDA Zone 4). It cuts through a 70' by 30' area of deciduous trees bordered by a section of lawn to the north and a stone wall and meadow to the south. The second path I helped make is within five acres of mature beech, maple, and oak woodland located nearby. The third path wends its way through a

100'-wide strip of steeply sloping woodland of mature white birch, hemlock, and maple that separates a main house from its guest-house on a New Hampshire hilltop.

Planning

A woodland walk is best designed among the trees, not on paper, because points of interest inherent in the woods — natural contours, rocks, trees, and water — provide clues to the direction the most varied path should take. The first points of interest to consider are those existing plants and rocks. In the five-acre woodland, for example, I found three 20'- to 30'-long lichen- and moss-covered rock outcroppings with ferns growing here and there in crevices; several close clumps of mature beech trees that suggested gateways or passageways, and a few rotted stumps that were hosts to natural miniature gardens of mosses, ferns and spleenworts.

Other points to consider are existing or potential views. On the New Hampshire hilltop, for example, I found that minimal clearing would open up a vista through beech trees and hemlocks to an 18th-century home on an adjacent hilltop.

Finally, look for pockets or areas of soil that are relatively root free, for these are places where new plants can easily be introduced. If you're lucky, you'll find a variety of soil conditions among those areas, for with variety of soil type comes the potential for a broad range of plants.

Marking

As you walk through woodlands looking for these points of interest, carry a roll of bright orange forester's tape with which to mark them. Once you have explored the entire area, go back to the outside of the woods to consider the starting and ending points of the path. The starting point can be suggested by a relationship to a door in the house, an existing pathway, areas of lawn, or breaks that exist or can be made in stone walls. For an endpoint, a path should offer a specific destination, such as a bench.

Once you know where the landmarks are in the woods and where the starting and ending points will be, you can begin to determine the exact layout of the path. Be careful not to be slavish in following the perimeter of the property, for you can end up with too many stretches of long, straight path. Curves and turns add suspense and draw the walker on.

Changes in direction are one way to vary the nature of a path. Changes in dimension are another. The trunks or branches of trees and shrubs on either side of the path can funnel closer and closer and then suddenly widen; tree branches above can also be left as is

or pruned to create different effects. I once high-pruned one group of 10 or so beeches 30' up, thus creating a lofty canopy in that area. At other places along that path, I pruned limbs to create an arch as low as 7', creating a more intimate feeling.

Distance between you and the point of interest is yet another source of variety. After passing within 2' or 3' of an intimately planted rock outcropping, you could come around a turn in the path to find yourself in a wide clearing, at the end of which is a dramatic view through the woods.

Clearing

Once a path is roughly laid out with tapes, you can begin three phases: First, I work its length, removing undergrowth and saplings and shovel or cut with a handsaw.

Next, if it is necessary, I work the length of the path with a chain saw, removing dead trees and taking out larger ones that either impede the smooth running of the path, block views, or confuse the image of more satisfying trees. Clearing small trees from the base of a magnificent birch can be like drawing a curtain back to reveal a vast sculpture.

Finally, I make a third pass with pruning shears and a handsaw to fine-tune the path. In one instance, I cleared between the trunks of several 150-year-old maple trees to open a view into a sheep meadow; at another point, I cut a window in saplings to frame a view of seasonal freshet. I also cut small saplings from along an old mossy stone wall, leaving the tumbled stones just as they were. Because the woodland in southern Vermont offered so many varied images, this one six-hour process completed the path. Someday I might add plantings, but for the moment the path looks attractive just as it is.

Other paths may not have that inherent appeal, so the next step is to decide where to introduce additional plants to provide areas of surprise or intimacy, screening or drama. New plantings need to look as natural as possible. To make them appear natural, I place them near existing landmarks such as boulders and rock outcroppings.

Improving the Soil

The soil is another consideration when siting new plantings. In many cases, I have found that woodland soil has been exhausted by ferocious competition for water and nutrients among existing trees and shrubs. In such cases, I look for areas where the ground is not too rooty: in relatively open spaces, in places near large boulders or rock outcroppings where roots have not yet penetrated, and in places where tree trunks have decomposed. I excavate the existing soil to a depth of 1' or more and then replace it with a mixture of one part topsoil, one part compost and one part peat. Lining the bottom of the hole first with woven plastic weed-barrier cloth helps keep the soil pockets free of tree roots.

For relatively root-free areas where the soil is not wholly depleted but needs enrichment, I fork the soil and then amend it. In clay soil I use one part sand, one part compost and one part topsoil; in sandy soil I use one part topsoil and one part compost.

I have also planted on, rather than in, rooty woodland soil by spreading an 8" to 10" layer of a soil-compost-peat mixture on top of the woodland floor and planting directly in that. Particularly, though, plants — hostas, Christmas ferns (*Polystichum acrostichoides*), maidenhair ferns (*Adiantum pedatum*), and *Woodsia* species, for example — can get a good hold on the soil this way before the surface roots of more aggressive trees get into the soil.

Adding Plants

Plants introduced along a woodland path should complement the beauty of the natural woodland. In one path, for example, I wanted woodland plants that would look natural and yet offer different points of interest throughout the year, so I planted shrubs and hardy perennials that could be found growing wild in the area. At the starting point, along curves, and at the endpoint, I planted one, three, or five witch hazels (*Hamamelis mollis*). Their yellow flowers appear in the late winter, and their handsome foliage adds a clear yellow to the image in autumn. In wetter areas I planted clumps of male and female winterberry (*Ilex verticillata*). Its brilliant red berries at the tips of 10' to 12' upright branches provide an accent from late autumn into early winter. I then underplanted these shrubs and the naturally occurring ones with a combination of trilliums, bloodroots (*Sanguinaria canadensis*), trout lilies (*Erythronium* spp.), Christmas ferns and foamflowers (*Tiarella*

cordifolia) to provide spring color and full-season foliage texture and color contrast. This was a simple planting that two of us finished in a morning, thus completing the path.

Larger paths may take several years to plant and mature, and that process, too, is part of the pleasure. In our woodland my wife and I planted an informal screen of deciduous shrubs to visually separate the lawn from the path. At the entrance to the path we set out a single wayfaring tree (*Viburnum lantana*). This drought-tolerant shrub matures at 6' to 7' and blooms white in early June. Bright-red berries follow shortly thereafter. Leaving a break of 6' or 8' to leave room for maturing plants, I then planted three arrowwoods (*Viburnum dentatum*) in a circle some 6' across. This shrub is airier and more upright than *V. lantana* and forms an 8' to 10' clump that blooms white in late spring. Next I planted five March-blooming witch hazels (*Hamamelis ×intermedia* 'Diana') in an irregular drift that broke up what could have become a too-perfect curve that followed the path exactly. This rangy, open-branched shrub blooms red in March and carries clear yellow leaves in autumn. Next came one lily-of-the-valley shrub (*Enkianthus campanulatus*). It blooms in late spring and has a growth habit that is more angular and upright. Thus it acts as a foil to the neighboring witch hazels and the next grouping of three sweet pepperbush plants (*Clethra alnifolia*). These clump-forming shrubs mature at 6' and carry highly fragrant blooms in August. I planted all of them in deep, compost-enriched soil; when mature, they will form a natural-looking 6' to 10' screen.

To mark the entrance to the walk, I set two 7' granite fence posts next to the first Viburnum *lantana* and on either side of the stepping stones at the beginning of the walkway. I then planted *Hosta* 'Frances Williams', interplanted with the daffodil 'Louise de Coligny', around one post. Near the other I chose plants that would provide color in early spring when many of the shrubs in the shrub screen were still in bud: a young *Magnolia stellata*, underplanted with *Bellis perennis*. For later color I planted *Phlox stolonifera* ('Bruce's White' and 'Blue Ridge') and *Dicentra formosa* 'Alba', in the midst of which rises the upright *Hosta* 'Krossa Regal'. Along the stone walkway I gathered combinations of other perennial plants that would offer color at various times of the year but would primarily create an interplay of foliage textures, shapes, and colors: *Bergenia cordifolia*, *Hosta sieboldiana* 'Elegans', *Epimedium youngianum* 'Niveum' and *E. ×rubrum*, *Pulmonaria angustifolia*, *Sanguinaria canadensis* 'Flore Pleno', *Dicentra spectabilis* and its white form 'Alba', and blue *Phlox divaricata*.

At the other end of the walkway, I planted a young *Stewartia pseudocamellia* opposite the group of three sweet pepperbush plants. I chose stewartia, a small tree, because it would form an upright, albeit living, counterpart of the granite fence post on the other side of the path. Furthermore, it would appreciate the cover provided by the neighboring trees in winter and would, as it matured, provide exquisite camellialike flowers and extraordinary rust-colored exfoliating bark. I then chose perennial groundcovers that would offer foliage interest and contrast with the stewartia and the pepperbushes: royal ferns (*Osmunda regalis*) and lower perennials such as *Phlox stolonifera*, *Bergenia cordifolia*, and *Hosta* 'Blue Cadet'.

The Path's Surface and Path Maintenance

Because our woodland path is so small, we were able to set stepping stones the length of it. The problem of covering longer paths is more easily solved: Let autumn leaves fall on them. They form a good mulch and an attractive, natural covering.

Maintenance of a path is simple. Each autumn cut back shoots or saplings that arise from stumps of trees and remove branches that have grown into the walkway. Mulch planted areas in fall with 2"–4" of compost for manure, and in the spring spread a 10-10-10 fertilizer on those same areas. Only a minimum of weeding is necessary.

A well-designed and -planted path provides years, even decades, of pleasure. And since it is relatively quiet, it offers a good place for contemplation. Yet at the same time it is dynamic and continuously changing: with the weather, with the seasons, with passing daylight, and with the growth of the plants. Because of these changes, the mood and feeling in a woodland walk are always different, thus ever engaging our imagination.

chapter three
PLANTS FOR SHADE

perennials, trees *and* shrubs
bulbs, corms *and* tubers

FROM THE WOODLANDS OF ASIA

by JOAN MEANS

By now, it has become a reflex: Need a plant for a shady place? Pop in a hosta, Japan's greatest gift to American gardeners!

There are, however, other options for gardeners who want more variety or who find that among the demure wildflowers of a naturalistic woodland garden, those mounds of highly puckered and variegated hosta foliage look as overdressed as a sequined dress at a church picnic. For some years I've been searching out bold herbaceous perennials to provide structure in my woods when the early "ephemerals" are past their prime. Although European hellebores and American umbrella leaf play their parts, I've discovered that, once again, Japan (along with neighboring regions in eastern Asia) is a major supplier of outstanding foliage plants for shady gardens.

Encouraged by the demands of an increasingly sophisticated gardening public, nurserymen are now offering many Asian woodland plants that once could be found only in the private gardens of collectors. At the same time, they are sponsoring botanical expeditions to look for plants in the wild and often they are taking a busman's holiday and going along, too. The sheer diversity of the exciting shade plants that are being discovered in newly opened regions of China and Korea, but also in the supposedly well-known forests of Japan, is amazing. Already available by mail order are exotic jack-in-the-pulpits; gingers with large, silver-veined leaves; and shade-loving peonies.

And it's becoming clear that there's much more to come. When Darrell Probst, a Massachusetts horticulturist and plant breeder, subscribed to an expedition to China a few years ago his return payment included a seed packet of mixed epimediums, woodland plants known in most gardens by only a few European representatives. But among the Chinese seedlings that Probst grew from that single packet, three have recently been confirmed by British authorities as species new to science. The most spectacular of these is a glossy-leaved, 8"-tall groundcover that boasts taller flowering stems each bearing up to 30 large flowers with sepals .5" wide and centered by a maroon cup and maroon spurs. The new epimedium, Probst announced, is to be called *Epimedium epsteinii,* honoring his "friend and mentor" Harold Epstein, an amateur gardener whose acre of woodland outside New York City became home to a world-famous collection of Japanese and Asian plants. Official word of the honor to Epstein arrived from British taxonomists only weeks before his death in 1997 at age 94.

It is fitting that, even as new gardenworthy plants are being introduced, Epstein should be recognized for inspiring generations of American gardeners to gain solid experience growing at least some of the woodland flora of eastern Asia. In recent years we have come to understand that these plants may be uniquely suited to life in the humus-rich soil of forested North America — that indeed, they sometimes share a common ancestry with our own native wildflowers, dating to the period before the two continents drifted apart on their tectonic plates.

As is true of our own wildflowers, discovering whether a plant will be cold-hardy or heat-tolerant isn't always a simple matter of matching latitudes. Who, for example, would expect to see a tropical begonia survive winters north of Boston? Yet *Begonia grandis* subsp. *evansiana,* an inhabitant of China south to Malaysia, has flourished in my USDA Zone 6 garden for years. The red-backed leaves are large and succulent like a rex begonia, and are carried on 2' stems topped by pink or white flowers in September. If ever a plant looked out of place in a New England woodland, this is it! Yet each time I try to move it new plants pop up from tiny tubers left in the old location. After seeing how this begonia has spread over a garden on the shore of Italy's Lake Garda, I imagine it could become a nuisance in southern areas where it has a chance to set seed.

No responsible gardener, of course, wants to see his plants jump the garden gate to invade the space of our native flora. Whenever I acquire a new species of suspect habits and hardiness, I keep it isolated for a year or two in a small trial bed or in a pot plunged in a cold frame. Aggressive self-seeders go to the compost heap, while plants of borderline hardiness, such as *Asarum splendens,* remain protected until divisions or cuttings prove able to survive in the open garden. This ginger is one of several newly introduced Asian species, and it is indeed splendid, with 12"-long evergreen leaves mottled in silver and enormous (for an asarum) 2"-wide flowers with white centers. As yet, I haven't found the right microclimate in my woods, but it should do fine in Zone 7.

Drifts of snow cover the ground of my pine-oak copse for much of the winter, so evergreen leaves are less important than they might be in gardens farther south. Nevertheless, if I'm going to give space to a foliage plant it has to earn its keep all summer without devel-

Glaucidium palmatum

Anemonopsis macrophylla

When out of bloom, *Anemonopsis macrophylla* looks much like a bugbane, but a forest of branching 3' stems appears in August, carrying a profusion of lavender flowers shaped like small, nodding Japanese anemones. These are best seen dancing in a large drift, backed only by the deep green of a large-leaved rhododendron.

oping slug-riddled leaves or keeling over into an early-August dormancy. Japan's jack-in-the-pulpits meet those criteria and are large enough to have real visual impact. Plant hunter Barry Yinger has introduced several *Arisaema* species that I haven't yet tried, but three other jacks get my slightly qualified "thumbs up." The best known of these is *Arisaema sikokianum*, which in May has spectacular purple-black spathes lined in white, centered with a white, knob-shaped "jack." In rich soil, plants may stand more than 2' tall and probably half of all seedlings will have silver streaks highlighting three-part leaves that can span nearly 2'. I find *A. sikokianum* especially effective when grown in large colonies between the pink-budded mounds of *Rhododendron yakushimanum,* a medium-size shrub with a summertime show of new foliage in shimmering silver.

The lesser-known *A. ringens* is slightly larger in all its parts. The broad leaflets look like shiny green vinyl; lurking beneath is a rather sinister green-and-brown-striped flower, fat and curved like a cobra's head. I like it rising above a lake of ground-covering *Primula kisoana,* a stoloniferous Japanese primrose blessed with rather large and hairy heart-shaped leaves that seem impervious to drought, disease and insects.

As for the exquisite *A. candidissimum,* I fell in love with it 20 years ago when I saw it growing in a Zone 4 garden. My love remained unrequited until only recently, when tubers finally became available in the United States. This jack has pale pink spathes almost like calla lilies and three-part foliage in which each leaflet is easily 1' wide and 14" long. Because it doesn't emerge until late in June, I find this arisaema especially useful planted among ephemeral wildflowers that go dormant early in summer — plants such as the Japanese *Adonis amurensis* which begins pushing up great yellow buttercups between snowstorms in February, elongates its stems clothed in filigreed leaves in April and May, and ends its season in June as a collapsed, yellowing heap.

If there's a problem with most of the other Asian foliage plants in my woods, it's not that they're difficult or require special attention — merely that they have yet to trickle down into the

an arisaema ILLNESS

Unfortunately, Asian jack-in-the-pulpits have a history of suddenly disappearing after a year or two, which understandably distresses growers who have shelled out several ten-spots for a single tuber. When this happened to Dr. Cliff Desch, a University of Connecticut biologist, he was able to pinpoint the culprit: a rust disease that is endemic, but not always lethal, to our own handsome native *Arisaema triphyllum.* Fortunately, the Asians usually survive until, in accordance with the strange sexual mores of many of this genus, the flowers have turned from male to seed-bearing female. If you can't or won't eradicate our native jack, the immigrants can be kept going (and the colonies increased) by gathering stalks of the brilliant red "berries" each autumn. The red flesh contains chemicals that inhibit germination (and are also highly irritating to the skin, making the use of plastic gloves imperative), so I put the squeezed-out seeds in nylon bags and hang them for a week in a toilet tank so that fresh water automatically washes over them a dozen times a day. The cleansed seed can then be sown in pots and left outdoors to germinate in the spring.

Paeonia veitchii

horticultural mainstream and consequently take some determination to track down. As Darrell Probst explains, "No matter how beautiful and easy to grow, plants will remain rare until customers learn to ask nurserymen for them."

Ah, there's the rub! When these plants have common names, they tend not to be English and their Latin monikers aren't always easy to remember, either. For example, there's the plant I bought as *Aceriphyllum rossii*. The maple-shaped, shiny leaves are 10" wide and stand on 9"-tall stems that are preceded in early spring by naked stalks bearing massive panicles of sparkling white flowers. In moist soil the gradually expanding mound of foliage makes an effective foreground accent among smaller plants such as hepaticas (which bloom at the same time) and the pink-and-gray fronds of the Japanese painted fern (*Athyrium niponicum* var. *pictum*). But now taxonomists say that Ross's mapleleaf must be called *Mukdenia rossii,* a forgettable name that may well doom it to horticultural obscurity.

Likewise with *Peltoboykinia watanabei*. Even I have to look for a label when visitors ask for the name of this plant. Again, the foliage looks as though it has been waxed, but the leaves are nearly circular and deeply cut into jagged lobes. In reasonably moist soil, each leaf measures 18" across and stands on a stalk at least as tall. The tiny yellow flowers, which appear on their own stalks in July, are nothing to swoon over, but they set copious seed that quickly turn a single plant into an effective groundcover in front of rhododendrons. Unwanted seedlings are easy to remove.

By contrast, everyone knows peonies, so why aren't the woodland species more popular in America? *Paeonia obovata* var. *alba* has flourished in the dappled shade of my woodland garden for 15 years. When this peony emerges in early spring, a coppery tone enhances the broadly lobed, graying leaves — a magnificent setting for large, white cups enhanced by golden stamens circling a crimson center. The flowers are fleeting, but the foliage remains quietly elegant during the summer months. As autumn turns the leaves to burgundy, large seed capsules open to reveal a fuchsia lining, corrugated like crushed velvet and studded with blue "berries."

A decade ago I returned from an English vacation with a root of *Paeonia veitchii* var. *woodwardii*, which, to my delight, produces an entirely different garden effect. The stems of this fast-growing peony support deeply cut, light green leaves arranged in a mound of weeping layers 2' high and a yard across, decorated in May by drooping pink cups. Not a true woodland species, *P. veitchii* comes from Chinese "yak meadows," which I take to mean that, transported to sea level, the plant needs some direct sun but also shade during the hottest hours of the day. In my woods both peonies produce self-sown seedlings that reach blooming size in three to four years. If they are rare, it must be because they lack a good publicist.

So does *Glaucidium palmatum*, a fair substitute for the fabled and difficult Himalayan blue poppy (*Meconopsis betonicifolia*). Actually a member of the buttercup family, Japan's lavender "poppy" is the bold-leaved plant I depend upon to flourish even in dry soil and deep shade. As the name implies, the lobed leaves are shaped like a hand, 14" across, and two are borne atop each 26"-tall stem. The flowers are usually a soft lavender, although white and deep purple occasionally appear. In my garden, they open in late April, a perfect counterpoint to yellow primroses.

It's curious that the islands that gave us *Acer palmatum*, the Japanese maple, are so rich in herbaceous plants with foliage shaped like hands or maple leaves. *Kirengeshoma palmata* is another of these plants, and when I began making a garden in my woods it was a rarity. Today it is widely available and is often recommended for its September crop of clear yellow, twisted bell flowers. But the strong, arching 3'-tall stalks carrying 7" lobed leaves can also add an architectural element to the woodland garden. Rather late to appear in spring, this is an excellent plant to fill the airspace above summer-weary primroses and those wildflowers that go dormant by June.

growing glaucidium FROM SEED

Although *Glaucidium palmatum* is often described in catalogs as an exceedingly rare plant, seed has long been readily available to members of the North American Rock Garden Society. My own plants came via that route; indeed, I killed my first batch of seedlings by trying to fertilize them into making true leaves. I've since learned that once the seed has germinated after a winter exposed to the elements, growth in the first year is primarily underground. The seedlings may need some mycorrhizal agent; they seem to do best when the undisturbed contents of a pot is gently decanted into a humus-filled hole in the woods. They are easily separated just after they've bloomed in their third or fourth year.

Also widely available is *Polygonatum odoratum* var. *pluriflorum* 'Variegatum', an elegant Japanese Solomon's seal that has such short rhizomes that the plant appears as a clump. The 24"-tall stalks are nearly upright and are clothed top to bottom with broad leaves delicately banded in white — a charming contrast to plants with much-divided foliage, such as *Cimicifuga japonica,* a bugbane that makes 15"-high mounds of compound leaves. The 2' wands of pink buds and white flowers appear in September.

Sometimes there is no substitute for a really big plant of statuesque proportions. In a woodland garden, where the massive columns of tree trunks must be visually related to the delicate leaves of ferns and wildflowers, the intermediary agent is often a large rhododendron. Where space is tight in my garden a rodgersia does the same job. Named in honor of a U.S. navy admiral who headed an expedition to Japan before the turn of the century, these plants of enormous dignity can reach massive proportions in moist soil. (With my gravelly soil I must be content with a mere 4.5'.) The bronzed leaves of *Rodgersia aesculifolia* are especially elegant: a whorl of eight leaflets, each up to 10" long and deeply quilted by veins.

For a while, *Astilboides tabularis* was a rodgersia and now it's not. No matter what it's called, however, I think of this awesome yet somehow comical plant as a cluster of soda-fountain tables. Balanced on a 3' stem, each round leaf is nearly flat, gently scalloped, 3' in diameter and colored a kelly green that is as shiny as baked-on enamel. To achieve its full potential the plant needs to be kept pumped up with plenty of water. Like so many objects with fine and simple lines, *A. tabularis* is wonderful on its own — by a pool, for example. But it can be put to more pedestrian uses, provided it has companions that can hold their own.

Lacking swampy land — but determined to grow this spectacular plant — I achieved an artificially high "water table" by burying a large tub, half filled with gravel before peaty soil was shoveled in, so the rim lies about 4" below the crown of the plant. Leo Blanchette, a local nurseryman who shares my enthusiasm for Asian woodland plants, says that a pinch of fertilizer once a month during the growing season helps encourage lushness. Is all this effort worthwhile? Hey, we're talking sculpture here, not just architecture!

To create a focal point at the end of a long grass path, I've planted these Chinese "tables" next to a *Hydrangea quercifolia* that flaunts large, oak-shaped leaves in the dappled shade of a katsura tree. In front there's a drift of *Hakonechloa macra* 'Aureola', one of Japan's finest plants for light shade. I first saw this magnificent

golden grass arching over the edge of a large container on Harold Epstein's terrace. Years later, it is still listed by many authorities as being 1' tall, but in fact this slowly spreading grass can, when set free in acid, humus-rich soil, easily reach twice that height.

An American hydrangea, a Japanese grass and a Chinese vegetative table, all growing together in a wooded garden north of Boston: they're a reminder of ancient connections to a world that was once, quite literally, one. As for the pioneering gardener who taught so many of us about Asian foliage plants, I think I'll remember him by planting some clumps of *Epimedium epsteinii.* Tribute, after all, should be paid.

Kirengeshoma palmata

THE SOARING CIMICIFUGAS

by C. Colston Burrell

Cimicifuga racemosa

Plant names tell stories that capture the imaginations of gardeners. The images conjured up by the name bugbane, however, are not necessarily pleasant. But the stately cimicifugas (the generic name derives from the Latin *cimex*, meaning bug, and *fugo*, meaning to flee or repel) are no bane to gardeners. Quite the contrary — they are a boon. That rare combination of elegance, adaptability and durability, traits they share with other members of the buttercup family (Ranunculaceae) such as clematis, delphiniums, hepaticas and columbines. (A word of warning: Gardeners should know that there has been a somewhat controversial name change. Recent taxonomic work by James Compton at the University of Reading, England, has transferred all bugbanes to the genus *Actaea*. Thus far, the nursery industry has not wholeheartedly embraced this change, so keep looking for these plants under *Cimicifuga* for now.)

One of the cimicifugas' most romantic names is wandflower. True, individual flowers of the wand have little to recommend them — they are but a cluster of straplike petals and stiff stamens. When collected together, however, they make a spectacular show. The flowers are followed by dry pods called follicles that contain flattened brown seeds. The seeds loosen in the splitting follicles and vibrate in the wind, giving rise to yet another common name, rattletop.

The foliage of all bugbanes rivals the flowers in beauty. The large, compound leaves are ternately divided — that is, they branch into three equal segments — and they may be subsequently divided up to three additional times, lending them a delicate, feathery look. Plants grow from stout rootstocks with eyes like diminutive peonies. Mature clumps form multiple, tightly packed crowns with congested foliage and a dozen or more wands of flowers. Cimicifugas are found in North America and in Eurasia. Like many plants with this dual distribution, the species diversity is richest in the southern Appalachians and in temperate Asia.

The American Species

North America is home to six species of bugbanes. The best known is black cohosh or cohosh bugbane (*Cimicifuga racemosa*; USDA Zones 3–9). A shallow creek wound lazily through the woods at the base of the slope where I first encountered black cohosh in the wild. Under a shadowy canopy of beech and oak, the tall spikes of fuzzy, ill-scented flowers towered over a delightful assortment of yellow lady's slippers, rue anemone, bellworts and ferns. At 5' to 8' tall, this plant is not for the faint of heart. Mature clumps sport multiple stalks that branch high on the scape like a pitchfork. The wands of white flowers open in mid-May or early June in southern regions, and into July in the North. The

Cimicifuga simplex 'Hillside Black Beauty'

Cimicifuga simplex var. *matsumurae* 'White Pearl'

Cimicifuga heracleifolia

Cimicifuga simplex 'Brunette'

leaflets of the thrice-divided foliage are deeply cut into ragged lobes. Its native range is from Massachusetts to Missouri and south to Georgia and Tennessee, though it has been widely planted in other areas.

Although American bugbane (*C. americana*; Zones 4–8) is smaller than black cohosh, they are nearly identical in foliage. Thankfully, two differences exist that make it simple to tell them apart. First, American bugbane blooms much later, in August and September. And second, each flower has two or more pistils, so multiple, long-stalked pods are found on each branch of the wand. A quick inspection of the dried stalks will set the record straight. Plants are native to rich woods in the mountains from Pennsylvania to Georgia.

The loveliest and least-known native species is Kearney's bugbane (*C. rubifolia*; Zones 4–8). It has long been sold as *C. racemosa* var. *cordifolia*, a name with no botanical standing. Plants are also commonly mislabeled in nurseries. If you get the real plant, you will know it right away. The leaves are twice ternately divided, with broad, shiny leaflets. The huge terminal leaflet is three lobed, heart shaped and coarsely toothed. In all, there are only three to nine leaflets, compared with up to 36 in the other species. Plantsman Graham Stuart Thomas aptly likens them to the leaves of Japanese anemone. The foliage forms a broad parasol only 2' above the ground, although in bloom the plant can reach up to 4'. The slender, branched spikes are gathered in a stiff, upright bunch at the center of the clump. In nature it is restricted to limestone coves in the mountains of Virginia, Tennessee and Kentucky.

Two additional cultivated species, *C. laciniata* and *C. elata*, are native to Oregon and Washington. Though eminently gardenworthy they have yet to gain wide distribution. Tall bugbane (*C. elata*;

Zones 4–8) grows 3' to 6' tall. The twice- to thrice-divided leaves have lobed, heart-shaped leaflets; flowers are borne in summer on leafy, sparsely branched stalks. Cut-leaf bugbane (*C. laciniata*; Zone 4–8) has a squat, many-branched leafy bloom stalk to 5' tall. The leaves have deeply incised, serrate leaflets, lending a delicate appearance to the open mounds of foliage. The plants bloom in summer.

The Eurasian Species

Two species, *C. dahurica* and *C. foetida*, are found as far north as the colder regions of Russia — good news for northern gardeners who may find them easier to grow than bugbanes from the southern United States. Dahurican bugbane (*C. dahurica*; Zones 3–8) is a charming plant with tight foliage mounds and tall, mid- to late-summer inflorescences that stick out from the main stem at every angle, giving the plant a startled look. Plants are dioecious; male plants have more lax inflorescences. The flowers are sweet scented. The foliage is two to three times divided, with toothed, ovate leaflets. The native range of this plant stretches from Siberia to Mongolia, China, Korea, and Japan. Fetid bugbane (*C. foetida*; Zones 3–8) has deeply lobed, serrate leaflets. This plant is seldom seen in America, though keen gardeners in Europe enjoy the sparsely branched, arching spikes of creamy flowers on 3' to 6' stems in late summer. Plants are native from Siberia to East Asia.

The hotbed of lustworthy bugbanes is temperate Asia, home of the popular autumn-flowering bugbanes, *C. simplex* and *C. ramosa*. They are very similar in all respects, though historically they have been considered separate species. (The current literature places *C.*

ramosa within the species *C. simplex*.) Autumn bugbane (*C. simplex* var. *matsumurae*; Zones 4–8) has two popular cultivars. 'White Pearl' has soft green leaves and pale green buds that open to fragrant, snow-white flowers in September and October. Plants are variable in height, as this selection is probably seed-grown. 'Elstead', which I first saw in Beth Chatto's extraordinary garden in England, grows to 3' tall and has striking purple-black stems. The purple-tinted buds open to pure white flowers. This choice plant is just now becoming available in this country.

The real lookers of the group are the purple-leaved forms of *C. simplex* (listed in the trade under *C. simplex* var. *simplex* or *C. ramosa*). Several cultivars are on the market, and each new introduction is an improvement over its predecessor. 'Atropurpurea' emerges a luscious, rich purple black in spring but as the leaves expand and temperatures rise it fades to light purple green, darkest along the edges of the leaves. The German selection 'Brunette' commands a hefty price at the nursery, but by midsummer is only slightly darker than 'Atropurpurea'. The color of both selections is highly dependent on temperature — hot nights slowly drain the purple coloration from the leaves. Unfortunately, from Virginia south, plants tend to fade to green and shed their lower leaves in the evening swelter. 'Hillside Black Beauty', selected at Hillside Gardens in Connecticut by Fred and Mary Ann McGourty, is the most colorfast selection to date. In trials by Wayside Gardens' John Elsley in South Carolina, plants retained their rich purple-brown color throughout the season. The flowers of all selections have a heady perfume that fills the garden in autumn when it is most appreciated.

The Sly Stallone of the genus is Komarov's bugbane (*C. heracleifolia*; Zones 3–8). Plants produce thick, arching 6' stems from open clumps. The flower spikes, which bloom in late summer and autumn, bend like shepherds' crooks. The six to nine three-lobed leaflets are thick and coarsely toothed. The leaves cluster at the base of the plant, making the lofty flower stalks all the more dramatic. This tough and attractive plant is found from Russia to China. The variety *bifida* has bold, twice-divided leaves.

These giants have some diminutive but dashing relations. Those with small gardens will appreciate the varieties of Japanese bugbane (*C. japonica*; Zones 4–8). These lovely autumn-flowering plants have ground-hugging foliage and slender, leafless, erect stalks of evenly spaced, starry white flowers. Unlike other species, the flowers are scentless. The taxonomic conundrum afflicts this group as well. Plants sold under the name *C. japonica* var. *acerina* (sometimes listed as *C. acerina*) have twice-divided leaves with up to nine palmately lobed leaflets. The stiff, sparsely branched, hairy bloom stalk rises to 3'. According to cimicifuga expert James Compton, this plant is actually a clone of *C. biternata* (Zones 3–8). More robust, with striking foliage, is the true *C. japonica*. The leaves have only three huge, broad, glossy, toothed leaflets. The showy, dense spikes of white flowers are carried well above the foliage in mid- to late autumn. Established clumps are quite dramatic.

Using Bugbanes in the Garden

Bugbanes are sensational garden plants of easy culture. As woodland wildings they prosper in a humus-rich soil that retains moisture throughout the growing season. They seem indifferent to soil pH as long as there is ample organic matter to buffer the soil. Plants tolerate a wide range of light conditions, although all species appreciate afternoon shade and in warmer zones require sun protection if they are to perform well. They are best sited in a partially shaded spot, with some direct light. They bloom well even in deep shade, but the flower wands may lean toward the light.

Few plants are easier to place than the bugbanes, since spikes are always needed for accent, especially in the shady garden. I grow most of the species and selections, and each has its appropriate spot. I use the tall, dense spikes of black cohosh like a gauze screen in a bed that separates my terrace from the neighbors' house. The erect stems accommodate low plants underneath the clump of leaves. About its feet a carpet of foamflower is punctuated with astrantias, wild bleeding heart, columbine and sedges. Nearby *Ligularia dentata* 'Desdemona' contributes the requisite bold foliage to contrast with the finely textured cohosh. Next to the June-blooming cohosh is one of the purple-leaved forms. Its September flowers extend the bloom season, and the dark foliage complements the rich red leaves of the ligularia. By placing this fragrant beauty near the terrace I can easily revel in the scent. In spring, when the foliage is at its richest hue, the sultry goblets of 'Queen of the Night' tulips make a suitably solemn display, enlivened by a carpet of the soft yellow *Aquilegia canadensis* 'Corbett'.

I have also seen purple-leaved bugbanes brilliantly used at Chanticleer, a public garden near Philadelphia. The wall of the shaded terrace is lined with a thick golden row of variegated hakone grass punctuated at even intervals by soaring clumps of bugbane. The effect is mouthwatering.

In my rear garden, a clump of 'White Pearl' bridges the gap between the canopy trees and the epimediums, trilliums and gingers below. The scent in autumn fills the air. I have placed a large patch of *C. biternata* in front of a drift of male ferns, whose fronds provide a restful complement to the coarse bugbane leaves in spring and summer and a lush backdrop for the September flowers. Kearney's bugbane, one of my favorites, forms a focal point at the end of a narrow path. The early-fall spikes jut up from an underplanting of epimediums and sweet woodruff. For a specimen, there is no better choice than *C. japonica*, with its huge, coarse leaves. My four-year-old plant, still an infant, will eventually fill a corner of the garden against a hedge of viburnums.

Despite their nomenclatural confusion, the bugbanes are an enchanting group of plants. I would be hard pressed to choose the best of the genus. Luckily, many species are available, so I do not have to. I can grow them all, and I do.

FERNS OF A DIFFERENT CUT

by SUE OLSEN

Christmas fern, sword fern, Goldie's fern, royal fern and maidenhair top a long and distinguished list of popular garden ferns.

These readily available species have consistently rewarded gardeners with a combination of ornamental appeal and reliable cold hardiness. But relatively few gardeners are aware of the ever-increasing selection of lesser-known U.S. natives as well as the extensive assortment of spore-grown imports that are now available. I'd like to recommend a few of the best. Always keep in mind, however, that ferns should never be collected in the wild. By making sure that the ferns you purchase are nursery propagated, you will help encourage an attitude of conscientious respect for our floral future.

North American Natives

Any collection of ferns would immediately acquire added luster by the addition of the Northwest natives *Polystichum braunii, P. andersonii* and the rare Alaskan *P. setigerum.* (The latter should not be confused with the British *P. Setiferum;* the spelling is similar, the appearance is not.) All are 2'- to 4'-tall evergreens whose new growth is covered with shaggy, silver scales that persist as rust-colored decorations as the fronds mature. *Polystichum braunii* (USDA Zones 3–8) has shiny, dark green, bipinnate (twice-divided) fronds that taper at both ends. *Polystichum andersonii* (Zones 6–9), by contrast, has less finely divided and less shiny foliage. It is distinguished, however, by the presence of a bulbil at the tip of each frond, which can be pinned to the ground in the autumn to produce a new plant the following spring. *Polystichum setigerum* (Zones 6–9) is both shiny and bristly, with a more upright habit. These robust species can be used in foundation plantings, as a backdrop for spring ephemerals or to lend unity and weight to shady mixed borders (all, in fact, thrive in woodland conditions).

There is also a wealth of smaller-growing native species. One of the most attractive, maidenhair spleenwort, *Asplenium trichomanes* (Zones 3–9), is a superior plant for the foreground of the partly shady rock garden. Its evergreen foliage clusters like green raindrops on brittle, black 8" stems. This species is easily cultivated in loose, well-drained soil. (The subspecies *quadrivalens*, which festoons Old World castle crevices and other mortared antiquities, appreciates a top-dressing of lime or broken concrete.) It has produced a

number of cultivars: 'Incisum' (or Incisum Group), with finely cut pinnules, and 'Cristatum' (or Cristatum Group), with the tiny fronds forking at the apices, are among the attractive alternatives for a petite niche.

The low-growing *Cheilanthes lanosa* (Zones 6–9) is more challenging, with its uncharacteristic preference for a sunny exposure. The fronds are on the bluish side of forest green, and as upright as a stand of conifers. This visual effect is the result of the fronds' covering of hairs — nature's way of preventing excessive transpiration. The ideal site for this cheilanthes is up against a rock, preferably on the leeward side with the fronds in full light, but the roots tucked under the rock for coolness and moisture. A mulch of pebbles around the fern's crown will help keep the roots cool and

Dryopteris erythrosora

prevent mud from splashing on the fronds during inclement weather. Good drainage is a must.

One superlative miniature fern for the shade has been beset with nomenclatural problems since its introduction in the Seattle area in the 1950s by plantsman Carl English. This is the dwarf maidenhair known as *Adiantum aleuticum* 'Subpumilum' (or *Adiantum pedatum* subsp. *subpumilum;* Zones 5–9); it is now classified by some botanists as simply a variant of this species. To distinguish it from the taller members of the complex, gardeners refer to it (without botanical authority but with conviction) as *A. a.* 'Subpumilum Type'. But whatever the name, it is a lovely little plant. The deciduous fronds, at once dense and delicate, are divided in the familiar five-fingered configuration, with the pinnae overlapping (imbricate) on small, black stems. The more light it receives, the more compact its habit. Full sun, however, will burn the foliage, especially when it is wet, so for best effect it should be protected from direct midday rays. It is as charming as it is variable, ranging in height from 3" up to 8".

Gymnocarpium dryopteris and its foliose variety, 'Plumosum' (Zones 3–8), add delicacy and charm to the moist woodland. Frequently seen in the company of *Cornus canadensis,* it is an appropriate nymph for a wildflower setting. It creeps about in woodland duff, sending up fresh, light green fronds throughout the season when its watering needs are met.

British Cultivars

For more than a century the British have provided horticulture with an extensive assortment of fern cultivars and varieties. Aided by the Victorian fern craze, every variant and abnormality was collected and propagated to meet an insatiable demand for something "different." As a result, there are dangled, bespangled, monstrose and other deviations, much as if nature went through her entire Baroque period while on holiday in Britain. Among this group are some first-rate plants. A good example is the popular *Polystichum setiferum* 'Divisilobum' (or Divisilobum Group) (Zones 6–9), which has often been saddled with the misnomer Alaska fern. Its soft, lax, 2' evergreen fronds form a beautiful pattern of finely divided tracery. It typically produces copious crops of bulbils along the frond's midrib that, if pinned down on organically enriched woodland compost, will produce a bevy of plantlets over the winter. This species, unfortunately, won't reliably survive where winter temperatures dip down to the single digits unless deeply mulched or blanketed with snow.

Among other British species, *Athyrium filix-femina,* the lady fern, has given rise to named variants in abundance. These are,

however, an uncertain lot, as the progeny are not stable and must be grown on for a number of years to determine whether they are truly ornamental or just "different." Some of the best potential candidates are in the "plumose" section — that is, they are furnished with exceptionally finely divided foliage, which gives them a feathery appearance. Equally distinctive is *A. f-f.* 'Frizelliae' (Zones 3–8), commonly called the tatting fern because of the resemblance of its minute pinnae to that form of handiwork. The late English authority Reginald Kaye described it as having "pinnae reduced to tiny lunulate or beadlike balls causing the fronds to look like a necklace of green beads." It is lower-growing than most of the "ladies." All the forms of *A. filix-femina* are deciduous, and are thus best suited to the summer garden or a site where the absence of foliage in winter will not detract from the landscape.

Not all ferns are feathery or for that matter even "ferny" in appearance. One example is *Phyllitis scolopendrium* (also known as *Asplenium scolopendrium;* Zones 5–9), the hart's-tongue fern, with kelly green, leathery, strap-shaped fronds. The American form of the species is both difficult and rare, but the European species, by contrast, is easy and common and has demonstrated a strong tendency to sport. It can claim parentage to some 400 cultivars, affectionately referred to as "scollies." *Phyllitis scolopendrium* 'Kaye's Lacerated', whose appearance hints at leaf lettuce, is one of the more common variants, growing to approximately 8". These evergreens prefer neutral to alkaline soil and benefit from a top-dressing of discarded eggshells or broken concrete.

Athyrium filix-femina 'Frizelliae'

Variations are also common among the British forms of the royal fern, *Osmunda regalis* (Zones 2–10). These primitive deciduous ferns have upright, locustlike foliage and, unlike most ferns, carry their spores on distinct stalks rather than on the underside of the frond. My favorite varieties are the undulate royal fern, *O. regalis* 'Undulata' (also known as 'Crispa'), a magnificent specimen with wavy margins that reaches a mature height of 4'. 'Purpurascens' is somewhat more subtle and not quite so tall. Its luminous, wine-colored new growth and purple stems distinguish it from the type, and it holds this glow well into the season. To display these varieties properly, they should be given ample room and a constant supply of moisture — just this side of a bog.

Choice Asian Ferns

While England may be the matriarch of fern culture, some of the best new introductions come from Asia. Two genera in particular, *Dryopteris* and *Polystichum*, have given contemporary horticulture some distinguished selections. *Dryopteris erythrosora* (Zones 6–8) displays beautiful coppery rose spring hues — a striking departure from the traditional ferny greens. In summer the red gives way to green, but any new fronds will be coppery. While variable in height, it usually reaches 30" and is an easy evergreen. *Dryopteris erythrosora* var. *prolifica*, also rosy, has smaller, more linear pinnae as well as propagable bulbils along the frond. Try them under a canopy of Japanese maples with a foreground of evergreen epimediums to unify the planting.

Evergreen *Dryopteris wallichiana* (Zones 6–9) presents a dramatically different appearance. Its emerging croziers are blanketed with conspicuous blackish scales that persist into adulthood and present a counterpoint to the fresh, apple-green tones of the spring fronds. Nevertheless, it can be somewhat unpredictable in severe cold weather. (I've had some freeze solid in 4" pots without a fatality, while the same arctic extreme killed a mature specimen in the ground!) However, it is well worth some pampering, as it makes a spectacular 4" specimen. If you are concerned about its hardiness, try planting it on the south side of the house (but in a shady spot). There it will be somewhat protected from the full force of cold north winds.

Dryopteris championii (Zones 5–9), by contrast, is a glossy evergreen whose emerging, silver-etched fronds are like a ray of sunlight in the forest. This new growth often appears alarmingly late in the season, often not until June. With lustrous mature fronds to 2.5', *D. championii* is an excellent choice to liven up the somberness of deep woods, especially when surrounded with the delicacy of wildflowers.

Lustrous foliage also characterizes my favorite polystichums. The tassel fern, *Polystichum polyblepharum* (Zones 5–8), which gets its common name from its arching new growth, has been the standard by which many new introductions are measured. At 2', this bestseller with its shiny fronds is an immediate attraction when placed in the garden, or for that matter the living room, where it is equally ornamental. It must not dry out, however, and does well when surrounded by moss, which will act as a living hygrometer, indicating the need for a drink before the fern suffers.

Polystichum makinoi and *P. neolobatum*, two recent immigrants from Japan, are leathery, forest green, 2'-tall evergreen aristocrats that look best when woven into a tapestry of matte foliage — hostas are excellent. The margins of *P. neolobatum* are stiffly bristled, so much so in fact that weeding around them is somewhat like pulling thistles from a juniper patch. *Polystichum makinoi* has softer bristles on squared pinnae tips and is very dark in color. Both of these species are suitable for Zones 5 through 9, and in my Zone 8 garden maintain a fresh appearance even when poking through the snow. All these polystichums, by the way, make excellent candidates for floral arrangements, where they will likely outlive the flowers.

Polystichum retrorsopaleaceum (Zones 5–9), which looks much like *P. braunii*, shows great promise as an ornamental giant for colder areas. A 2'- to 3'-tall robust evergreen, it is one of the first to appear in the spring. The unfurling fronds display a profusion of

Adiantum aleuticum 'Subpumilum'

translucent, inward-curving, straw-colored scales that persist on the mature foliage.

Asia has its share of maidenhairs, too, including a pair that should beguile even the most fern-resistant gardener. The graceful *Adiantum aleuticum* 'Japonicum' (Zones 5–8) displays the traditional five-fingered, pedate, maidenhair shape, but has the added attraction of brick-red new growth. It is also easier to cultivate than our native East Coast *A. pedatum* (it isn't fussy about soil or a magnet for slugs), and makes a fine, airy, 2' addition to woodland plantings. It is completely deciduous, but does not defoliate until well after the first frosts. Not all maidenhairs are deciduous, however, and one of the most highly recommended species, the Himalayan maidenhair (*A. venustum;* Zones 5–9), makes a wonderful evergreen groundcover. It, too, has a hint of red in its young foliage, but it is lower growing, to 12", and the elfin fronds are triangular rather than pedate in outline. Once established it spreads easily, but never aggressively; in fact I am always wishing for more.

This is but a sampling of the many choices the gardener has when selecting ferns, whether for use en masse in the woodland or as specimens in the collector's corner. They offer subtle variations in color and yet create a coherent design with their greenery. They can be bold and architectural or small and delicate; prostrate or plumy; deciduous or wintergreen. They cool us with the refreshing suggestion of a walk in the woods or the splash of a brook, calming the garden as well as the soul.

Polystichum makinoi

fern TERMS

APEX (PL. APICES): the tip of a pinna or pinnule

BIPINNATE: doubly or twice divided

BLADE: the expanded part of a frond

BULBIL: a small bulblike structure capable of rooting

CRESTED: having tips that are repeatedly forked

CROSIER: a young, coiled frond

CROWN: the point from which a cluster of fronds rises

FIDDLEHEAD: another term for crosier

FOLIOSE: leafy

FROND: a fern leaf

IMBRICATE: overlapping, like shingles on a roof

INDUMENT: a covering of hairs or scales

PEDATE: palmately divided

PINNA (PL. PINNAE): the primary division of a frond

PINNATE: having undivided pinnae on both sides of the rachis

PINNATIFID: cut almost to the rachis

PINNULE: a secondary division of a pinna

PLUMOSE: feathery in appearance

RACHIS: the axis, or central "stem," of the frond's blade

SCALE: a small, thin, membranous outgrowth

SPORANGIUM: a small organ that contains spores

SPORE: the reproductive cell of a fern

STERILE FROND: a frond that does not produce sporangia

STIPE: the stalk of a fern leaf

THE NEW LOOK OF CORALBELLS

by ANN LOVEJOY

Each May, my morning coffee-break stroll through the garden puts me in mind

of a sentimental song we sang in grade school.

It had to do with lilies-of-the-valley, now in full, fragrant bloom, and white coralbells that only ring when the fairies sing. Though not audible and only just coming into bud, my coralbells are undeniably lovely. They will remain so well into autumn, for unlike the old-fashioned coralbells of the song, my contemporary heucheras are valued more for their extraordinary foliage than for their floral charms. Indeed, for both plant fanciers and colorists, hybrid foliage heucheras are one of the hottest developments in modern gardening.

Actually, their floral charms are nothing to sniff at, for many of the new coralbells bloom as long and hard as their forebears, sending up several sets of slender, elongated stalks tipped with airy sprays of small, nodding bells over the course of the summer.

Still, even when abundant, the flowers of these new hybrids are often less showy than their leaves, which are their crowning glory for much of the year.

This new look for a cottage garden favorite is the result of patient hybridizing between a number of modestly attractive species, most of them North American. Oregonian Dan Heims has been a pioneering force in this effort, and his striking introductions are snapped up as quickly as they appear in nurseries and garden centers. Heims's hybrids are belles indeed, some dramatically beautiful, others downright brazen. They delightfully amplify offerings from breeders in the Midwest and the South, notably the former Montrose Nursery in North Carolina, whose *Heuchera* 'Montrose Ruby' (*H.* 'Palace Purple' × *H.* 'Dale's Strain') is the grandmother of many of today's most remarkable hybrids.

Because these recent hybrids often owe their distinctive foliage patterning to our native woodland species, they prefer light or partial shade and may show signs of distress — browning, scorched, or curling leaves — in full sun, particularly in hot climates. Move the sufferer into a cooler spot and keep it moist and you should see healthy new growth appearing within a few weeks. Indeed, where the old

Heuchera 'Ruby Veil'

Heuchera 'Pewter Veil'

Among colorists, the current favorite purple is 'Chocolate Ruffles', a sumptuous creation with large, rounded leaves. When young, their lobed edges are deeply ruffled, but older ones have a looser flounce. The leaves are copper pink when young, maturing to dark chocolate with burgundy veins and undersides. (The similar 'Ruby Ruffles' has slightly lighter foliage.) Deep red flower stems nicely set off the white flowers, making a pleasant echo for upright spumes of foxy red *Carex buchananii* or the lacy snowflake leaves of *Geranium sanguineum* 'Album'. 'Chocolate Ruffles' makes a smashing underskirt for the shrubby St. John's wort, *Hypericum androsaemum* 'Albury Purple', whose young foliage has a similarly murky cast. To emphasize the pewtery luster of the coralbell's undercoat, tuck in a few clumps of wallflowers such as *Erysimum* 'Joseph's Coat' and *E.* 'Wenlock Beauty', whose flowers vary from

coralbells are troopers, blooming well even under imperfect conditions, the foliage hybrids require consistently moist, humus-rich, and slightly acid soils to look their best. Most form 1'-high mounds threaded in season with numerous 14" to 18" flower stalks, though happy offspring of *H. americana* can reach 3' in height and spread close to 2'. Unless otherwise noted all are hardy to USDA Zone 4.

The first of the foliage coralbells to make horticultural headlines was *H. micrantha* 'Palace Purple', which has ruddy leaves and white flowers. (At least it should; quite often flats of inferior seed-grown plants are offered instead of divisions of the true plant.) 'Palace Purple' was a chance seedling discovered in England when seed of several North American native coralbells was being grown near the Queen Mother's personal garden (thus the palace part). Though its parentage is still argued, this enormously popular plant is generally accepted as being a spontaneous garden hybrid of the silver-netted northwesterner *H. micrantha*, probably crossed with *H. americana*, a softly dappled southeastern species.

Queenly as it is, 'Palace Purple' is cast in the shade by more recent hybrids, many of which combine rich coloration with contrasting veination as well as scalloped and ruffled leaf edges. Indeed, new coralbells are proliferating in such numbers that they threaten to overwhelm the market with a bewilderment of forms. Some, such as the glimmering, glossy 'Plum Puddin', have dark red or purple leaves. Others, such as the shimmering 'Smoky Rose', are silvery green, often streaked with pink and lavender and usually dappled or marbled with gray. A few, such as 'Whirlwind', are marvelously textured and ruffled. Just as with hostas and daylilies, however, many coralbells are so similar as to be indistinguishable.

Heuchera 'Chocolate Ruffles'

Heuchera 'Ruby Ruffles'

buff and amber to lavender and purple above slender, blue-gray foliage. The fuzzy matte green pleats of lady's-mantle (*Alchemilla mollis*) contrast happily with the glossy coralbells, as do the huge, long-fingered leaves of Korean *Angelica gigas*, sea green infused with burgundy. The massive flower heads of the angelica — like outsize Queen Anne's lace — are a rich, chocolate red, one step darker than that of 'Chocolate Ruffles' coralbells.

To play up the brighter pinky red of shaggy peonies or old roses, sultry 'Ruby Veil' is the pick of the crop. This one has baroquely shaped and textured leaves of dusky red with fuchsia veins and backsides. Its rosy flowers bring out the red highlights in *Euphorbia dulcis* 'Chameleon', a dusky little spurge with upright new shoots and sprawling flowering stems that explode into puffy thunderclouds of bloom. Where most euphorbia bracts are lime green, these are murky shades of black and gray and slate and wine, taking on hotter tints of bronzed red and tawny orange by late summer.

This changeable spurge also makes a stunning companion for a midnight-dark coralbell, *H. americana* 'Velvet Night'. Its youthful leaves look like black velours, taking on the coloration of 'Concord' grapes as they mature — deep purple bloomed with gray.

A quietly potent beauty, *H.* 'Pewter Veil', has subtly patterned leaves that emerge copper red, then pass through several shades of bronze, red and plum as they age. When mature, the leaves are heavily washed with lead gray and veined in forest green, with hot pink undersides. Frosty green *H.* 'Mint Frost' is another subtle stunner whose tinsel-trimmed leaves seem to reflect light into dark corners of the shady garden. Both partner admirably with deer ferns (*Blechnum spicant*) and cool blue *Hosta* 'Krossa Regal' in a shady site.

Where sun and shadow are mingled 'Pewter Veil' can nestle near a cascading *Sedum* 'Vera Jameson', which begins the season looking blue, then blooms in frosty shades of plum, lavender and mauve. To round out the picture, tuck in cheerful *H.* 'Coral Cloud', a sun lover whose glowing mist of salmony flowers persists for most of the summer.

Most understated of all is *H. americana* 'Dale's Strain', a compact plant with delicate pink flowers and heart-shaped, marvelously marbled foliage. When young, the leaves are a matte chartreuse with olive-

green markings, while mature ones are silver green with spruce veins. It does best in light shade and moderately moist, rich soil.

A shady spot is also best for *H.* 'Snowstorm', a lusty plant whose big, rounded leaves, heavily dusted with clean white spots and spatters, can scorch in full sun. Its bright red flowers look like little firecrackers against the cool backdrop of its leaves, which make a wonderful counterpoint to broad-bladed hostas such as the little, heart-shaped 'Blue Cadet' or plain green *H. plantaginea*, with its sheaves of fragrant white flowers.

In my new garden, a gathering of coralbells creates a mosaic on the forest floor beneath towering cedars and Douglas firs. Punctuated by tall sheaves of *Ligularia przewalskii*, native false hellebore (*Veratrum viride*), and evergreen huckleberries, the coralbells spread in subtly patterned pools. Here grow several clumps of the majestic *H.* 'Eco Magnifiolia', bottle green burnished in silver and veined with wine. Near it shimmers its seedling, *H.* 'Sterling Silver', its lustrous leaves veined in chilly blues and purples. These deepen the purple red of *H.* 'Montrose Ruby', whose dull red leaves are laced with threads of gunmetal gray and silver.

Along with these foliage hybrids grow clumps of native heucheras, both *H. micrantha*, a dainty species with softly mottled leaves and dusky pink flowers, and *H. cylindrica* (Zone 3; to 30"), with flowers the color of creamy jade. This is the parent of the delicious 'Greenfinch', a selected form whose marbled, ice-green leaves are topped with thickly studded stems of chartreuse flowers.

Heuchera 'Palace Purple'

I have added a group of foamy bells, or heucherella (Zone 5; to 2'), a bigeneric hybrid involving *Heuchera brizoides* and its cousin *Tiarella cordifolia.* The most commonly grown form is *Heucherella alba* 'Bridget Bloom', which boasts glazed and scalloped leaves and burgundy-brown stems tipped with deep pink flowers in cloudy clusters. These days, a crop of cousins are appearing, including Heims's handsome *H.* 'Crimson Cloud', a blowsy billow of hot red flowers. To set it off add a ruffle of *H.* 'Snow White' (Zone 5; to 18"), the first clean white heucherella. This dainty creature also looks at ease among native plants, and makes a charming companion for subtly colored coralbells such as *Heuchera villosa* (Zone 6; 2'), with large, deeply lobed leaves and masses of buttery blossoms.

Once you begin collecting coralbells, it can be hard to stop. To reduce the expense, try sharing with friends. Coralbells become large plants in just a few seasons, and mature plants can be divided in spring or fall by removing the central, woody core of an older plant and replanting the smaller chunks that fall away during the process. If you are drawn to experimentation, save seed from special forms or species and grow your own. Spring-sown seed produces plants that are garden-ready in autumn. Their delightful diversity of form and color will be apparent almost as soon as the seedlings are visible — indeed, a flat of baby coralbells is an enchanting sight. It is great fun to select the most attractive forms, which can be massed in shady areas to create a magical carpet of leaf and flower. And who knows, your pet coralbell may one day be grown in gardens all over the country, as ubiquitous as the great 'Palace Purple'.

Heuchera 'Snowstorm'

LADY'S SLIPPERS FOR EVERYONE

by CAROL BISHOP MILLER

The lady's slipper (*Cypripedium* spp.) is to a gardener what cheesecake drizzled
with chocolate is to a dieter: a prescription for failure and guilt.

For, more often than not, when one of these temperamental native
terrestrial orchids is transplanted to the garden it enacts a slow,
torturous death scene, shrinking year by year into oblivion.

The commonly accepted explanation for this phenomenon is
that lady's slippers acquire their soil nutrients through a symbiotic
association with a root fungus of the genus *Rhizoctonia*, and that by
removing the plant from its natural environment this essential relationship is terminated, and the plant slowly starves to death.
Indeed, the myriad, microscopic, wind-borne seeds of the lady's
slipper perish upon germination unless the fungus is at hand to
invade and nurture the dividing cells for up to two years before
the plant emerges from the ground. Once the seedling begins
photosynthesis its dependence upon the fungus lessens, though it
continues to benefit from the relationship indefinitely.

Bill Cullina, nursery manager and propagator at the New England Wild Flower Society's Garden in the Woods in Framingham,
Massachusetts, has published an intriguing article suggesting that
root damage may be to blame for transplant failure, at least for the
pink lady's slipper (*C. acaule*). According to Cullina, the brittle,
fleshy roots, which spread horizontally from the crown for 12" to
18" through the well-oxygenated humus layer above the mineral
soil, cease to grow and are rendered vulnerable to rot when
their tips are cut or broken. Also, if the plant is not replanted properly — that is, with its roots outspread beneath a thin cover of leaf
mold — it will suffocate.

Blooming in spring or early summer, the pink lady's slipper,
or moccasin flower, whose pink-veined, pouchlike lower petal, or
labellum, resembles a ballerina's slipper, is quite tolerant of dry
conditions but demands a very acid soil pH of 4.0 to 4.5. Here in
my stomping ground, northern Alabama and central Tennessee,
colonies are found on sandstone under pines and hemlocks. In acid
bogs it seeks hummocks, where the roots are bathed with humid air.

The large yellow lady's slipper (*C. parviflorum* var. *pubescens*) is
an easier garden subject, favoring moist, humusy soil in a wider, less
acidic pH range — between 5.0 and 8.0. Around here it inhabits
limestone hillsides canopied with beech and other hardwoods.
There is something cartoonish about its flower, with its bright
yellow, 2" balloonlike labellum framed by a pair of corkscrew side

Cypripedium kentuckiense

petals that are speckled and streaked with green or brownish
purple, and a pair of pointed sepals forming a matching cap and
collar. The flowers are carried singly or in pairs at the tips of 6" to
28" scapes bearing pleated leaves. The small yellow lady's slipper (*C.
parviflorum* var. *parviflorum*) has smaller, more fragrant flowers
and needs constantly moist, moderately acid soil rich in hardwood
leaf mold.

Similar in culture to *C. p.* var. *parviflorum*, the spectacular
lady's slipper (*C. kentuckiense*) sports a flower with a scalloped
labellum the size of a hen's egg, in white, cream or yellow. Noted for
its heat tolerance, it is particularly recommended for the South.

In the garden, plant lady's slippers shallowly in loose, organic
soil of the proper pH for the species. They need more light (two to
four hours of morning sun is ideal) and less water (excessive water
invites rot) than most gardeners provide. Should they live, reward
them with a twice-yearly snack of diluted houseplant food or composted cow manure. Be careful with fungicides and other strong
chemicals near lady's slippers, and note that touching these plants
causes skin irritation in some people.

A few researchers and growers are gaining expertise in the patient
art of propagating lady's slippers — good news for the dwindling
wild populations pressured by overcollecting and habitat loss; less re-
assuring, perhaps, for the remorseful gardener hovering by the
deathbed of a persnickety cypripedium.

JAPANESE ANEMONES FOR LATE SUMMER

by THOMAS FISCHER

It's late August, and the garden is not a pretty sight. The peonies and irises are long gone, the daylily foliage looks like hell, and the late-blooming asters haven't kicked in yet.

You feel sorely tempted to get rid of all the garden tools in the next yard sale and take up needlepoint. Then you come to the clump of Japanese anemones you wisely planted a year ago last spring. They didn't amount to much that first season, but now they've had time to settle in a bit. The mound of foliage, consisting of handsome, three-lobed, dark green leaves and rising to a good 3', breathes the freshness of spring. Hovering above on slender stems, the unopened buds resemble green- or pink-tinted pearls, while the 3" flowers, with their silky petals and ring of golden stamens, carry themselves as elegantly as a demimondaine of the belle époque. (After all, many selections did originate in late 19th-century France.) To top it all, the display will probably go on for more than two months. Maybe it's not quite time for that yard sale.

Although *A. hupehensis* var. *japonica* also bears the common name of Japanese anemone, it is the cross between this plant and *A. vitifolia*, dubbed *A.* ×*hybrida*, that has given us the range of cultivars — from single to fully double, and from white to deep crimson pink, with varying admixtures of purple — that comes as such a welcome respite at this time of year. While the doubles can be quite cheerful, I confess to a preference for the singles, or near singles, and for the paler colors. The two I grow are the exquisite, shell-

Anemone ×hybrida 'Konigin Charlotte'

pink 'Königin Charlotte' ('Queen Charlotte') and the equally beautiful 'Honorine Jobert', in pure white. Any moderately fertile, well-drained soil suits them, and they prosper best in a bit of shade. If these plants have any faults, it is that they are reliably hardy only to USDA Zone 6, and that once established they have a tendency to spread — sometimes with alarming speed. If you find it painful to witness these displays of force majeure in the border, try planting them among spring-blooming shrubs such as spireas and deutzias — not only do they look splendid against a solid green background, but they also add color and interest to an otherwise monotonous scene. Because Japanese anemones don't establish well in the fall, it is essential to plant them only in spring, and it's a good idea to mulch them their first winter (and every winter thereafter, if you live in the northernmost part of their range). Once they get going, however, there's no need for further worry — these true garden classics will be blooming long after we've shed our own petals.

at a GLANCE

TYPE OF PLANT: herbaceous perennial **FAMILY:** Ranunculaceae **HEIGHT AND SPREAD:** 3' to 5½' **LEAVES:** palmately compound, with three ovate lobed and toothed leaflets, slightly hairy underneath **FLOWERS:** 2" to 3" across, single to fully double, white to medium violet purple, with prominent boss of golden stamens **BLOOM PERIOD:** August–October, depending on the cultivar **HARDINESS:** USDA Zones 6–10 **PROPAGATION:** by 2" root cuttings taken in fall and laid horizontally in pots or trays, then lightly covered with potting mixture; division is rarely successful and seed is sparse or absent **CULTIVARS:** 'Andrea Atkinson', large single white; 'Elegans' ('Max Vogel'), semidouble pale purple violet; 'Honorine Jobert', single white; 'Königin Charlotte', semidouble clear pink; 'Kriemhilde', single deep pink; 'Loreley', semidouble pearly pink; 'Margarete' ('Monterosa'), double reddish violet; 'Richard Ahrends', single pale violet purple, tepals irregularly shaped; 'Whirlwind', semidouble, green-flushed white **COMPANIONS:** *Aconitum* spp., *Cimicifuga* spp., *Clematis* 'Kermesina', *Rosa glauca* **PROBLEMS:** none serious

EPIMEDIUM ADVENTURES

by C. COLSTON BURRELL

I am a lustful gardener. I once referred to myself as a chlorophyll addict, and an earnest voice asked who had bestowed my certification. Though I joked that she had obviously missed my swearing in at the White House, I am in fact self-certified.

Epimedium versicolor 'Sulphureum'

One of my merit badges was surely acquired by growing epimediums. This comely genus in the barberry family (Berberidaceae) is related to favorites such as mayapple (*Podophyllum* spp.) and twinleaf (*Jeffersonia* spp.), but epimediums have their own unique charms — and new species continue to be discovered. Of the 54 currently recognized species, at least 20 have been named in the last 10 years, and the mountainous regions of central China are still yielding new species (which are being promoted by enthusiasts like Darryl Probst).

Though I am always adding new epimediums to my collection of 300-plus clones, it is difficult for me to play favorites in a genus with dozens of flower shapes and sizes in a rainbow of colors. I love them all. I want them all. I'll get them all! In the area of my garden I call the torture chamber, stalwarts like *E. pinnatum* subsp. *colchicum* and its hybrid *E.* ×*perralchicum* thrive in poor soil and dense shade with no supplemental watering. Graceful curved stalks sport outfacing yellow flowers arrayed like lily-of-the-valley.

to do
IN THE GARDEN

1. Remove all the old epimedium foliage before new growth starts to emerge. Nothing spoils the show like a tangle of brown leaves. Likewise, nothing is more frustrating than trying to trim out old leaves after the new ones emerge. Buds invariably get damaged or snipped off.

2. Mulch beds early to avoid burying emerging bulbs and perennials. Use a light leaf mulch or compost rather than heavy bark, which swamps the crowns of most perennials, robs the soil of nutrients, and can encourage fungal diseases.

3. Use containers of bulbs to enliven dull spots in the garden where late-emerging perennials are planted.

'Frohnleiten' and 'Wisley', two of my favorite selections, keep company with *Helleborus odorus*, wood anemone (*Anemone nemorosa*) and hardy cyclamen.

Heading my list of favorites among the new introductions with yellow flowers is *E. ecalcaratum*, with nodding, floppy bell-shaped flowers slightly reminiscent of kirengeshoma. It weaves through a planting of maroon toad trilliums (*T. cuneatum*), which shares its April bloom period. Much showier in flower and foliage is *E. franchetii*, with large, spear-shaped leaflets and flowers with long, curved spurs like spiders. *Epimedium lishih chenii* and *E. chlorandrum* are variations on the theme. I use these as a mixed groundcover under stout clumps of yellow-flowered fairybells (*Disporum uniflorum*) and ferns fronting a drift of yellow-leaved bleeding heart (*Dicentra spectabilis* 'Gold Heart').

More subtle and charming is the early-blooming *E. pubescens*, with airy sprays of tiny flowers like a swarm of white mosquitoes over mottled, evergreen leaves. The main show comes in March, but expect repeat bloom through June. On a gentle slope next to a well-traveled path, I have paired it with the bold foliage and waxy flowers of *Trillium simile* over a carpet of delicate Himalayan maidenhair (*Adiantum venustum*), and the effect is stunning. *Epimedium stellulatum* 'Wudang Star' has flowers

wonderful EPIMEDIUM COMPANION

European wood anemone, *Anemone nemorosa*

Starry light blue to white flowers carpet the ground like snow in early spring. This denizen of open woods adapts beautifully to gardens in North America. Spidery shoots push from the cold ground, opening five oval sepals that close and droop in the cool of the evening, revealing a faint blue blush on the reverse. Plants grow 2" to 4" tall from creeping rhizomes that look like slender pretzels. Plant in rich, humusy, evenly moist soil in full sun to light shade. Crowded clumps flower poorly, so divide as plants go dormant. USDA Zones 4–8.

twice the size of most and looks great with black-flowered hellebores and a carpet of white glory-of-the-snow (*Chionodoxa luciliae* 'Alba').

This spring, I'll be enjoying all of these combinations, and, with the help of Probst's epimedium specialty nursery, Garden Vision, fawning over more new prizes destined to become favorites.

CARPETS OF BLUE PHLOX

by THOMAS FISCHER

One of the most pleasing features of the genus *Phlox* is that it has something for everybody: tall, opulent selections for the border; mats, buns and tuffets for the rock garden and a handful of delightful, spring-blooming species for woodland conditions.

Blue phlox (*P. divaricata*), a member of this last group, occurs over a huge portion of the eastern United States in fertile wooded areas that receive abundant winter and spring moisture. (In fact, it will even tolerate full sun, provided the soil never dries out.) Anyone lucky enough to have come across blue phlox in the wild will realize that it is meant to be seen en masse. The plants form spreading mats of prostrate stems that root at the nodes. In late spring, the erect flower stems erupt into a cloud of fragrant, blue-lavender blossoms. (There are also a couple of outstanding white clones: 'Fuller's White', with deeply notched petals and heat- and humidity-tolerant 'Eco Notchless White'.) Whether you choose a blue- or white-flowered form, plant as many as the available space will allow — an isolated plant or two will look merely pitiful, whereas a good-size patch will create a sea of delicate color from which islands of creamy foamflower or vivid azaleas can emerge.

at a GLANCE

TYPE OF PLANT: herbaceous perennial **FAMILY:** Polemoniaceae **HEIGHT:** 12"; subsp. *laphamii*: 12" to 15" **HABIT:** forms loose, spreading mats, rooting at nodes **LEAVES:** medium green, ovate-lanceolate to oblong, 1.25" to 2" long, semideciduous **FLOWERS:** usually lavender blue, .75" to 1.5" across, with a notched, five-lobed corolla (unnotched in subsp. *laphamii*), held in loosely branched clusters, fragrant **BLOOM PERIOD:** late spring **NATURAL RANGE:** Quebec south to northern Georgia, west to Michigan; subsp. *laphamii*: Minnesota and Wisconsin south to central Georgia and eastern Texas **HARDINESS:** USDA Zones 4–9 **CULTIVARS:** 'Clouds of Perfume', pale blue; 'Dirigo Ice', pale blue; 'Eco Blue Moon', exceptionally full pale blue; 'Eco Notchless White', heat-tolerant; 'Eco Texas Purple', dark purple with a red-violet eye; 'Fuller's White'; subsp. *laphamii*, deep blue lavender with unnotched petals **PROPAGATION:** by seed or division; named clones must be propagated vegetatively **COMPANIONS:** *Athyrium* spp., deciduous azaleas, *Carex* spp., *Cypripedium calceolus*, *Milium effusum* 'Aureum', *Paeonia mlokosewitschii*, *P. obovata* var. *alba*, *P. veitchii* var. *woodwardii*, *Tiarella* spp., *Trillium* spp. **PROBLEMS:** Powdery mildew on the leaves, especially in hot, humid areas (cut back affected parts). Also, rabbits love to nibble on the plants.

Much confusion exists over the popular plant sold as *P.* 'Chattahoochee', variously described as either a clone of *P. divaricata* subsp. *laphamii* or as a hybrid with *P. divaricata* as one of the parents. But several years ago, Georgia nurseryman Don Jacobs proposed a solution. Apparently, the original 'Chattahoochee' came from a group of unnotched, red-eyed *P. divaricata* clones collected by Mrs. J. Norman Henry in the late 1940s near the Georgia-Florida border; these plants, however, have not been in commerce for many years. According to Jacobs, plants that bear the name 'Chattahoochee' today are actually hybrids of *P. amoena* (also called *P.* ×*procumbens* 'Variegata') and *P. subulata* or *P. pilosa* or else a selection of *P. pilosa* subsp. *fulgida*. All of which is no doubt good to know, and need not interfere in the least with our appreciation of the charms of *P. divaricata* in any of its named or nameless forms.

CHARMING, DURABLE FRINGED BLEEDING HEART

by THOMAS FISCHER

One bright May morning, a few years ago, I was strolling through the garden with a friend who
had just been bitten by the gardening bug and was eager to learn more about plants.

As we wandered by the shade borders, something caught her eye. "What is that exquisite little fern with the blue-green foliage?" she asked. I really can't excuse what I did next; something just came over me. "Oh, that?" I replied airily. "Lovely, isn't it? The Latin name escapes me for the moment, but it belongs to a terribly rare genus of ferns."

"Wait a minute — what are those little pink flowers? It's covered with them!"

"Why, it's blooming! They only do that, you know, when cultural conditions are absolutely perfect."

"But I read somewhere that ferns are nonflowering plants." I thought I could detect a steely glint of mistrust in her eyes.

"Well, that's what they'd like you to think. Oh, just look at those peonies!" And I hustled her off to another part of the garden.

Suffice it to say that the plant in question was no fern at all, but rather fringed bleeding heart *(Dicentra eximia),*

a charming and durable perennial found in hilly wooded areas throughout a wide stretch of the Northeast. The 1'-tall clump of finely divided, long-lasting, glaucous foliage does resemble some dainty fern (thus tempting one to invent whoppers for unsuspecting visitors), but of course the display of heart-shaped flowers gives the show away. While these flowers are much narrower than those of common bleeding heart *(Dicentra spectabilis),* they are produced over a much longer period and come in a range of tints from the usual rosy pink to pure white. (White-flowered forms tend to have plain green rather than glaucous foliage.) Dappled shade, humusy soil and an even supply of moisture will

at a GLANCE

TYPE OF PLANT: herbaceous perennial **FAMILY:** Fumariaceae/Papaveraceae
HEIGHT AND SPREAD: both 1' to 1.5' **LEAVES:** basal, 4" to 12" long, finely incised and fernlike, usually gray green **FLOWERS:** 1" long, narrowly heart-shaped, magenta to rosy pink (rarely white), borne on 2' scapes **BLOOM PERIOD:** April/May–October **NATURAL RANGE:** New York Alleghenies south to Tennessee and North Carolina **HARDINESS:** USDA Zones 3–10 **CULTIVARS:** 'Alba', white; 'Snowdrift', pure white; 'Zestful', medium pink **HYBRIDS:** 'Adrian Bloom' deep pink; 'Bacchanal', deep ruby; 'Bountiful', purplish red; 'Langtrees', cream and pink; 'Luxuriant', cherry red, blooms profusely; 'Stuart Boothman', ruby pink, plant compact, foliage blue green tinged with purple **PROPAGATION:** readily self-sows; seed sown in spring requires cold stratification; named varieties can be divided in spring **Companions:** *Aquilegia* spp., *Geranium maculatum, G. sylvaticum, Hosta* 'Blue Moon', *H.* 'Halcyon', *Iris gracilipes, Lunaria annua* 'Alba Variegata', *L. rediviva, Paeonia mlokosewitschii, P. obovata, Smilacina racemosa* **PROBLEMS:** Aphids are occasionally a bother.

keep the plant in bloom from May to October, and in suitable conditions it will seed itself about freely. Dry spells are apt to cause it to go dormant, although it will revive the following spring.

The West Coast equivalent of *D. eximia* is *D. formosa*. Although the two are quite similar-looking, *D. formosa* is said to be more tolerant of dry soils but less tolerant of hot, humid summers. Along with *D. nevadensis* and *D. peregrina*, these two species have spawned a brood of delightful hybrids, some, like 'Bacchanal' and 'Bountiful', with sumptuous, ruby-tinted flowers. My very favorite, however, is 'Langtrees', with ivory flowers just touched with pink, forming a subtle symphony with the intensely blue foliage. A close second is 'Stuart Boothman', whose crimson flowers nestle against leaves that blend blue green with purple in much the same way as *Rosa glauca*. All of these hybrids will spread if given the chance, but I have yet to meet the gardener who thought they were a nuisance. And just in case you were wondering, I did finally fess up to my friend. And ferns never, ever bloom.

RING IN BELLWORT

by THOMAS FISCHER

The beauty of our eastern woods in spring owes more to the lily family than to any other group of plants.

Just think of the liliaceous gems to be found among *Erythronium, Polygonatum, Smilacina, Trillium* and *Lilium* itself, to name but a handful of genera. For poise and delicacy, the bellworts rank with the finest of these plants, and the best of the bellworts, *Uvularia grandiflora*, has few rivals even among the most regal trilliums or trout lilies. From a creeping rhizome, the slender stems emerge in early spring, the narrow, perfoliate leaves furled at the tip like an umbrella. The leaves free themselves once the stems reach about 6" in height; a few more inches of growth and they begin to arch, revealing long, narrow buds that open into drooping, shuttlecock-shaped flowers in a clear lemon yellow. These look splendid next to companions with blue or white flowers, though it is hard to think of any plant they wouldn't flatter. After flowering the stems continue to grow and the leaves continue to enlarge, until at maturity the plant forms a 2.5' leafy clump. Ordinary woodland conditions suit *U. grandiflora* — that is, light shade and moist humus-rich, well-drained soil. In the wild *U. grandiflora* occurs in areas with calcareous soil, and some authorities recommend adding lime to the planting hole. It has seemed perfectly happy, however, in the acid soil beneath an oak tree in my own garden. Light supplemental feedings with a balanced fertilizer will produce more robust, floriferous clumps, which will show to best advantage this bellwort's distinctive blending of vigor and grace.

at a GLANCE

TYPE OF PLANT: herbaceous perennial **FAMILY:** Liliaceae **LEAVES:** medium green, ovate to oblong-lanceolate, to 5" long, pubescent beneath **FLOWERS:** solitary, slender, nodding, bell-shaped, lemon yellow, to 2" long **HEIGHT:** 8" to 1' when in bloom; ultimately to 2.5' **BLOOM PERIOD:** April–May **NATURAL RANGE:** southwestern Quebec west to Minnesota; south to Tennessee and Oklahoma **HARDINESS:** USDA Zones 3–9 **SIMILAR SPECIES:** *U. perfoliata:* flowers smaller and paler; *U. sessilifolia:* flowers smaller, greenish yellow, leaves not perfoliate **PROPAGATION:** division in spring or early fall; seed possible but slow **COMPANIONS:** *Anemone nemorosa, Brunnera macrophylla, Cardamine trifolia,* epimediums, *Jeffersonia dubia, Phlox divaricata,* evergreen polystichums, pulmonarias, *Trillium grandiflorum, T. luteum* **PROBLEMS:** none serious

SHARP SEDGES

by C. COLSTON BURRELL

Sedges are the invisible "ornamental grasses." Their subtle beauty is often overshadowed by showy miscanthus or stately molinias.

But the tough, adaptable sedges — which are not true grasses at all, but rather belong to a separate family, the Cyperaceae — deserve a second look. They excel in places where grasses seldom succeed, including partial shade, while offering the same fine texture and graceful motion that make grasses indispensable. You can put sedges to work in a variety of landscape settings, from containers to low-maintenance groundcover plantings. Some can even be used as a no-mow substitute for turf.

The genus *Carex* — which contains most of the cultivated sedges — numbers over 2,000 species. They venture into every conceivable ecosystem, from tundra to tropical rain forests. In a prairie, for example, much of the green that we see is in fact predominantly sedges. Grasslands and savannas offer a wealth of sun-loving, often drought-tolerant species. Woodlands harbor their own gardenworthy species. Wetlands are yet another major ecosystem exploited by sedges. Although most sedges have specific habitat niches, in cultivation they are adaptable to a wide range of conditions. Despite heat and drought, they always look crisp and tidy. And though few sedges are as tough as common grasses like miscan thus, when properly sited they are quick to establish and long lived.

Carex morrowii 'Ice Dance'

Carex comans 'Frosted Curls'

Designing with Sedges

A well-grown sedge provides a garden with season-long texture and distinctive form. Ranging from linear and threadlike to boldly strap-shaped, sedge foliage also comes in a remarkable array of colors, from chartreuse to nearly black and may be striped or banded in white or brilliant yellow. Many species have attractive, albeit subtle, flowers in spring or summer. Most have an upright, vaselike form, though some species form a tight, dense groundcover perfect for filling gaps between more vertical plants.

Use small, fine-textured sedges between pavers or to soften the edge of a patio. Contrast them with the bold leaves of hostas, bergenias, rodgersias or ligularias. Use upright, vase-shaped, or widely arching selections to add height and variety to dull groundcover plantings.

Sedge leaves catch the light and seem to glow when backlit by the sun. The increased popularity of water and bog gardening provides a huge canvas to be painted with colorful selections such as Bowles' golden or San Diego sedges.

Sedges for Various Settings

Most sedges are shade tolerant and thus ideal for woodland gardens. I like to use variegated selections to brighten the shadows. Bedrock comes to the surface in a few spots in my woodland garden, and since rocks and sedges look great together I have placed a number of sedges, either singly or in clumps, atop the outcroppings or within the rock crevices to create a cascading effect. One of my favorite combinations involves a drift of creamy variegated woodland sedge (*C. siderosticha*

Carex dolichostachya 'Kaga Nishiki'

DESERT-ISLAND SEDGES

1. Fringed sedge (*Carex crinita*) excels in soggy sites and water gardens in sun or shade. Once you try it, you'll wonder why it's not widely grown. Light green leaves form a mounding, fine-textured clump. The only drawback to this beauty is that it is deciduous and flops pitifully with the first frost.

2. *Carex dolichostachya* 'Kaga-nishiki' is a relatively new introduction. It has foliage that is fine textured and soft, unlike many sedges which are either stiff, wiry or both. Plants grow well in rich soil in light to full shade.

3. I wish I could produce the huge chartreuse clumps of Bowles' golden sedge (*Carex elata* 'Aurea') that I see in England and the Pacific Northwest. But even in my hot, dryish conditions here in inland Virginia, this beauty makes a rounded, fine-textured clump of glowing yellow leaves. It grows best in standing water in rich soil with full sun or light shade.

4. In my garden, *Carex flagellifera* is the best of the "dead sedges." It has been longer lived than others and has a rich, ruddy bronze color with a hint of green. Plants grow in moist soil in full sun and form mop-headed clumps of hairlike leaves.

5. The stiff but gracefully arching deep green leaves of Gray's sedge (*Carex grayi*) form attractive clumps in light to full shade. In late spring the flower heads emerge and transform the plant into a work of art, with knobby inflorescences that look like clusters of medieval maces.

6. The long, slender blades of variegated black sedge (*Carex nigra* 'Variegata', or 'On-line') all seem to lie in the same direction, and the clump sways in the breeze like a bed of eel grass when the tide is high. The subtle yellow edges of the gray-green leaves add a bit of class to spots with open shade.

7. Crisp, precise, and beautifully variegated describes the foliage of *Carex oshimensis* 'Evergold'. Unlike most variegated sedges, this one sports narrow leaves with a central yellow stripe bordered by green margins. (Most other variegated sedges have leaves edged in the lighter color.) The neat clumps are decidedly aristocratic.

8. The crisp, leathery leaves of drooping sedge (*Carex pendula*) form an arching clump worthy of the Trevi Fountain. In summer, tall stalks rise above the leaves, dangling their green inflorescences like worms on a hook. Plants are fully evergreen in warm zones and turn gold when frost arrives. Performs equally well in water or average garden soil in sun or shade.

9. With palmlike stems topped with whirligigs of dashingly variegated blades, the utterly dazzling *Carex phyllocephala* 'Sparkler' belongs in every garden. It is borderline hardy for me in Virginia, so I grow it in a container kept frost free and slightly moist in winter.

10. The flat, knifelike blue leaves of *Carex platyphylla* look fabulous anywhere. I've tried plants from several locations, but most were a bit touchy and did not thrive. However, Dale Hendricks of North Creek Nursery has introduced a selection from southern Pennsylvania that is vigorous and easy.

11. From the moment I laid eyes on the blades of *Carex siderosticha* 'Variegata', beautifully striped in creamy white, I knew it would be a favorite. The blades quickly expand to form a clump that some visitors mistake for a narrow-leaved hosta. A superb and easy plant that thrives in rich soil and shade.

12. I saw Fraser's sedge (*Cymophyllus fraserianus*) growing in the wilds of the Smoky Mountains before I ever tried to grow it. The leathery, black-green leaves formed a perfect accompaniment to the fuzzy white flowers making this the most handsome of the woodland sedges when in bloom.

In contrast to grasses which have jointed stems with the leaves arising from knobby nodes, sedges have unjointed, triangular stems. The sheath of each leaf arises from the crown rather than from a node along the stem, and the overlapping sheaths give strength and support to the flowering stems. In cross section (right), sedge stems are triangular — you can feel three distinct edges if you run your fingers up the stem.

Since sedges are wind pollinated they offer no showy petals to attract pollinators. The inflorescence consists of short spikes and smaller segments called spikelets, which hold the individual flowers. The spikelet is densely packed with flowers and each flower has a single scale. Each flower, and later the fruit, is enclosed in an inflated structure called a perigynium which gives the sedge spike a beadlike appearance. Some species have separate male and female spikes where the male appears as an extension or tail on the inflorescence. Many sedge inflorescences are accompanied by leafy bracts that can be quite showy.

Carex phyllocephala 'Sparkler'

Carex oshimensis 'Evergold'

Carex elata 'Aurea'

Carex conica 'Snowline'

Carex comans 'Bronze'

'Variegata') in front of a large patch of primrose-yellow *Epimedium epsteinii* for a subtle echo, and is then jazzed up with some orange-yellow celandine poppies (*Stylophorum diphyllum*). For contrast I added drifts of blue woodland phlox (*P. divaricata*).

Bold sedges have a place in the garden, too. Fraser's sedge (*Cymophyllus fraserianus*), which grows in the dry, dense shade of hemlock forests, takes tolerance to an extreme. I added its spreading mounds of deep green, strappy leaves to an unirrigated portion of my garden with the upright thick-stemmed wood fern (*Dryopteris crassirhizoma*) to hold the spot among summer-dormant anemones at the base of a spreading 'Prinavera' witch hazel. In another part of the garden deep blue-gray *Carex platyphylla* makes a great groundcover at the base of a redbud, backed by the deep purple flowers and mottled leaves of wake-robin (*Trillium cuneatum*).

The so-called dead sedges of New Zealand add a unique coppery color to sunny perennial beds or conifer gardens. Their tufted to vase-shaped forms combine beautifully with the silver of artemisias such as beach wormwood (*A. stelleriana*) or *A.* 'Powis Castle'. I have a large drift of *Carex flagellifera* underplanted with deep purple-leaved coral bells (*Heuchera* 'Plum Pudding') and backed by orange *Agastache* 'Firebird', which ignites the sedge's bronzed leaves to create a stunning combination.

One of the most innovative uses for sedges is as a lawn substitute. They can take light foot traffic, and only need mowing once a year. Pennsylvania sedge (*Carex pensylvanica*), for example, will form a dense, lawnlike groundcover in the dry, root-infested shade of mature sugar maples. On the West Coast, nurseryman John Greenlee is promoting the local native carex as a lawn substitute for his region.

Gardeners are only now beginning to discover sedges, so the hardiness of many species hasn't been fully determined. Some may prove hardier than their ostensible ratings indicate, provided they are well mulched or receive consistent snow cover. Experiment! The uses for sedges are limited only by your imagination. Take a second look at them and you'll discover many distinctive sedges to add variety and elegance to your garden.

BOTANICAL/COMMON NAME	ORIGIN	HABITAT	USDA ZONES
Carex albula (C. comans)/curly hair sedge	New Zealand	W, MF	7–9
Carex baccans/crimson-seeded sedge	India and China	W	8–10
Carex buchananii/leather-leaf sedge	New Zealand	G, W	7–9
Carex caryophylla 'The Beatles'/'The Beatles' sedge	hybrid origin		7–9
Carex comans 'Bronze'/New Zealand hair sedge	New Zealand	G, W	7–9
Carex conica 'Snowline'/miniature variegated sedge	Korea & Japan	F	5–9
Carex crinita/drooping sedge	North America	W	2–8
Carex dolichostachya 'Kaga-nishiki'/Kaga brocade sedge	Japan	F	5–9
Carex elata 'Aurea'/Bowles' golden sedge	Europe	W	4–8
Carex flacca (C. glauca)/blue sedge	Europe	G, W	4–9
Carex flaccosperma (C. albursina)/broad blue sedge	North America	MF	6–9
Carex flagellifera/bronze hair sedge	New Zealand	W	7–9
Carex grayi/Gray's sedge	North America	G, MF	3–8
Carex morrowii/Morrow's sedge	Japan	MF	6–9
Carex muskingumensis/palm sedge	North America	W	3–9
Carex nigra/black sedge	Europe	MF, W	4–8
Carex ornithipoda 'Variegata'/birdfoot sedge	Europe	DF	7–9
Carex oshimensis 'Evergold'/'Evergold' sedge	Japan	MF, W	7–9
Carex pendula/pendulous sedge	Eurasia	W	5–9
Carex pensylvanica/Pennsylvania sedge	North America	DF	3–8
Carex phyllocephala 'Sparkler'/'Sparkler' sedge	Japan	W	7–10
Carex plantaginea/plantain-leaf sedge	North America	MF	4–9
Carex platyphylla/broad-leaf sedge	North America	F	5–8
Carex siderosticha 'Variegata'/variegated woodland sedge	China, Japan	MF	3–9
Carex spissa/San Diego sedge	North America	W	7–9
Carex stricta/tussock sedge	North America	W	2–7
Carex testacea/dead sedge	New Zealand	G, W	6–9
Cymophyllus fraserianus/Fraser's sedge	North America	MF	6–8
Rhynchospora colorata/white-top sedge	North America	W	7–9

Habitat key: DF = dry forests; G = grasslands; MF = mesic forests; W = wetlands

DESCRIPTION

Grown for very fine texture, can be used as annual in the North; 'Frosted Curls' has white-striped leaves

Stiff, glossy foliage accented by stunning red flower spikes; tall and dramatic; limited hardiness

Most commonly available of the bronze-leaf group; upright, fine-textured clump

Moppy heads of dark green, short leaves; makes a fine-textured, tight groundcover in light shade

Good in containers where its brown color shows up better; a wet-meadow species but tolerates dryness

Fine-textured species forming a spreading vase shape from a tight clump; fine white edge to the leaves

Similar to *C. pendula* but deciduous and extremely cold tolerant; pendulous, catkinlike flower structure

Beautiful, fine-textured vase shape, yellow to cream stripes

Upright, clumping, with bright chartreuse leaves edged in green; handsome in wet or dry sites; light shade

A running species for sun (shade in the south); bright gray-blue, narrow foliage

Blue-gray evergreen foliage, shade and drought tolerant; underutilized and hard to locate

Very fine-textured "dead sedge"; forms a spreading vase; leaves shorter than *C. comans*

Bright green, arching to erect leaves, decorative flower heads like medieval maces; a prolific self-seeder

Bold, stiff, wide leaves form an open vaselike clump; 'Goldband', 'Ice Dance' (Zone 4),
and 'Variegata' are variegated selections

Bog plant adaptable to garden conditions; needs half-day of sun; spreads by runners to make open
clumps; 'Oehme' has yellow-edged leaves

Sea-green to grayish leaves longer than *C. glauca;* 'Variegata' has a subtle gold edge; sun or shade

Low, spreading vase shape; forms tight clumps in light shade

Good for brightening a shaded spot; creamy variegation is down the center of the leaves, unlike other sedges

Strapping, glossy, evergreen leaves in arching clumps to 4'; showy, drooping catkinlike inflorescence

Clumping to running, fine textured; tolerates dry soil and root competition; good lawn substitute

Forms umbrellas of boldly white-striped leaves and fuzzy terminal flowers; plain green wild form also grown

Wide, evergreen, puckered leaves; drought tolerant; yellow-green flowers in spring; attractive groundcover

Broad blue leaves in a tight clump, gorgeous and drought tolerant

Similar to *C. plantaginea;* tolerates dry shade, bleaches in hot sun; two new cultivars are 'Island Brocade'
and 'Spring Snow'

Similar to *C. pendula;* upright, coarse texture; blue-gray leaves, evergreen; grows in water or wet soil

Clump forming in standing water but will run in drier soil; 'Variegata' is a yellow-variegated selection

Rounded, arching form; fine-textured "dead sedge"; hardier than others

Broad, ribbonlike, dark evergreen leaves; white flowers in early spring; tolerates deep shade; needs acid soil

Showy, snow-white bracts below the inflorescence; needs consistent moisture for best growth

MAGNIFICENT MAHONIAS

by CAROL HALL

*Handsome in flower, fruit and leaf, these underused
evergreen shrubs keep their good looks all year.*

Mahonia ×media

Flowering broad-leaved evergreen shrubs are unexcelled for providing all-season interest. Rhododendrons, pieris, camellias, laurustinus, skimmias, aucubas, evergreen azaleas and all the rest rightfully deserve all the coddling, pampering and winter protection they require in all but the mildest climates. But one genus in this highly prized category goes a giant step further: *Mahonia*. Sure, the year-around visual interest is there. All species exhibit handsome, leathery, pinnately compound, holly-like leaves, fragrant yellow flowers that bloom early (some in midwinter) and showy summer berries. But with forms ranging from treelike to groundcover, uses ranging from the visually sublime to the homey and practical and native habitats ranging from mild and moist to exposed and dry, there's bound to be a mahonia for every garden.

All this variety is found in a mere handful of species. With a few exceptions, mahonias will tolerate a wide range of soils, climates, exposures and conditions. Excluding the magnificent Asian species, whose hardiness is typical of most flowering broad-leaved evergreens (USDA Zones 7–8), mahonias are cold hardy to about –20°F. And they're sun tolerant in all but the hottest climates.

They're also fuss-free: no deadheading, no special soil preparations, no spraying, no pruning, no regular watering or fertilizing necessary once they're established. Even snow isn't a problem. Like true hollies, mahonia's spiny leaves tend to deflect snowflakes, thus preventing heavy buildups that can cause breakage. If a stem does get broken through accidental mishap, it can simply be pruned to a side branch or even to the ground. All mahonias sprout from old wood and are fast growing, so even old specimens rejuvenate easily.

The Pacific Northwest Natives

I come by my bias toward mahonias honestly. My husband and I, having lived in the Pacific Northwest for a combined total of 104 years (and gardened there for nearly as long), can't imagine gardening without them. And no wonder. Of the handful of mahonia species that have transcended their provincial origins to become popular in gardens around the world, three are native to the Pacific Northwest.

The first and most important of these is Oregon grape (*M. aquifolium),* sometimes called Oregon holly grape in acknowledgment of its glossy, dark green spiny leaflets. This tall (to 6' or more), slowly suckering shrub is common in river valleys, coastal areas and open woodland west of the Cascades, and is the state flower of (where else?) Oregon. The givens of Oregon grape (besides the foliage) are upright woody stems, clustered yellow flowers from March to May and grapelike clusters of blue-black edible berries in July and August.

Plants in the wild exhibit a striking degree of variation: they may be 3' tall and spreading in exposed or drier areas, or 8' tall and almost vinelike in moist, shaded woodland. Likewise, the winter foliage may turn dark purplish brown or reddish purple, or remain green with the odd leaf of fire-engine red. New growth may be bronze, pink, orange or purple red. As you might expect, at least half a dozen named cultivars exist, each with its own appeal.

Mahonia nervosa is even more widespread in the wild. There's nothing at all nervous about this good-looking, low-growing groundcover ("nervose" actually means prominently veined) that spreads by means of underground runners. In fact, you'd be hard pressed to find any wooded area between British Columbia and California where this species did not colonize some portion of the forest floor. Sometimes known as low Oregon grape, this species is better described by its other common name, longleaf mahonia. Its leaves may be up to 18" long, which in many cases is more than the plant's height. The neatly paired, notched (rather than spined) leaflets are not glossy like those of tall Oregon grape, but are more likely to turn color in winter — purple, orange, brownish or bright clear red. The spring-blooming flowers are held in long racemes and the berries that follow are decorative, abundant and edible.

Although *M. nervosa* was introduced to garden cultivation in 1822 — one year before *M. aquifolium* — it has a narrower range of adaptability, and so is not nearly as widely planted as its taller cousin. Partial shade, acid soil, spring moisture and a humusy soil texture are all necessary, although plants will tolerate full sun in cool-summer climates. Summer drought is easily handled in semi-shaded sites.

The other Pacific Northwest native is more commonly found on the eastern, drier side of the Cascades. *Mahonia repens,* or creeping mahonia, is rapidly becoming popular as a tough and versatile low shrub for massed plantings, low-maintenance groundcover in sun or shade and evergreen understory where dry shade is a problem. This species closely resembles *M. aquifolium* but on a more reduced scale: shorter height (2' to 3'), fewer and shallower leaflet spines, smaller flower clusters and less abundant (but just as edible) fruit. It does sucker much more freely, eventually making dense patches, but is never invasive, since unwanted shoots are easily removed.

The Asian Mahonias

Half a world away from the Pacific Northwest are the Asian mahonias. Although the family resemblance to their western counterparts is unmistakable, the main appeal of these less cold-hardy shrubs is their architectural structure and foliage. *Mahonia japonica* and *M. lomariifolia,*

Mahonia nervosa

Mahonia japonica Bealei Group

both natives of China, are the most widely grown, along with their hybrid, *M. ×media*. All three are large, many-stemmed plants that can easily reach the size of small trees, and all bear majestic leaves, which, in the case of *M. lomariifolia*, may be 2' long and bear as many as 23 pairs of neatly symmetrical spiny leaflets.

The winter-blooming, fragrant yellow flowers of the Asian species are held in 1'-long, usually lax racemes that open from the base outward over many weeks. The large blue berries that follow are unusually decorative, being held in long, prominent sprays. But even without flowers or berries their satiny foliage would stand out in any garden. In *M. japonica* 'Hivernant' some leaves turn yellow, orange or red, especially in fall and winter. *Mahonia ×media* cultivars display dark, shiny, blue-green foliage all winter. Even the huge, shrimp-colored leaf buds of these species are noteworthy, resembling large, exotic beetles.

Caring for Mahonias

Mahonias need little or no attention beyond the occasional removal of an overly tall or gangly old stem. However, a top-dressing of compost every few years will keep both plants and soil in good condition. A generous planting hole containing bone meal and back-filled with soil enriched with rotted manure or compost will get new plants off to a healthy start. On sandy soils plants will appreciate a drink or two during very dry weather.

Insects of any kind are rarely a problem, although a few leaves may be notched by vine weevils if these pests are present in large numbers. Diseases are similarly rare. In humid climates leaves may show a physiological spotting by winter's end, but these will soon be replaced by fresh growth.

The only conceivable downside to mahonias is that if your area experiences wet Augusts, you may end up with more seedlings of *M. aquifolium* than you bargained for. August is usually bone dry in our garden, but after one freakish rainy summer we found thousands of seedlings the following spring. The solution? Harvest the berries and make jelly before they become overripe and fall to the ground.

TYPE OF PLANT: broad-leaved evergreen shrubs **FAMILY:** Berberidaceae (barberry family) **HARDINESS:** most North American species USDA Zones 4–9; most Asian species USDA Zones 7–9 **EXPOSURE:** partial shade optimal (most are sun tolerant); protect Asian species from desiccating winter winds **SOIL:** well drained, reasonably fertile **PLANTING DEPTH:** top of root ball 1" to 2" beneath soil level for shrubs; just beneath soil for groundcover types **PLANTING TIME:** March–May or September–October **WATER NEEDS:** drought tolerant when established **FEEDING:** established plants need little or none **PROPAGATION:** species by ripe seed in August; hybrids and cultivars by leaf cuttings in September–October **PROBLEMS:** none serious

SPECIMENS: Since these Asian shrubs can reach the size of small trees they need rich, moist soil. Best displayed as one-of-a-kind focal points. These are the least cold-hardy species (0–10°F/USDA Zones 7 and 8), so they are best sited in sheltered locations protected from cold or dry winter winds. As an extra precaution, wrap the lower stems and crowns of younger, more vulnerable specimens in burlap for winter.

BOTANICAL/COMMON NAME: *M. japonica* (leatherleaf mahonia) **CULTIVARS/COMMENTS:** Bealei Group (more erect and compact form; fragrant flowers; hardiest of the Asian species); 'Hivernant' (shorter than species at 6' × 6'; foliage exhibits bright color in fall and winter) **SIZE/HABIT:** 8' × 8', rounded

BOTANICAL NAME: *M. lomariifolia* **CULTIVARS/COMMENTS:** Early-winter flowers; less cold hardy than *M. ×media* hybrids **SIZE/HABIT:** 10' × 8', upright and arching

BOTANICAL/COMMON NAME: *M. ×media* (hybrid of *M. japonica* and *M. lomariifolia*) **CULTIVARS/COMMENTS:** 'Arthur Menzies' (compact, upright habit); 'Charity' (stately form; fragrant early-winter flower sprays); 'Winter Sun' (free-flowering; form similar to 'Charity') **SIZE/HABIT:** 8' × 8', arching

GENERAL LANDSCAPING: These hardy species are versatile garden workhorses, happy in sun or shade, moist or seasonally dry climates, acid or alkaline conditions and in sandy or well-drained clay soils. Excellent in mixed-shrub borders and massed plantings. They also make fine stand-alone specimens and are even suitable for large containers. Use in formal settings (foundation plantings, entryways, hedges and screens) as well as naturalized, native or wildlife gardens.

BOTANICAL/COMMON NAME: *M. aquifolium* (Oregon grape, Oregon holly grape, tall Oregon grape) **CULTIVARS/COMMENTS:** 'Apollo' (vigorous Dutch form; large, deep yellow flowers); 'Atropurpurea' (winter foliage rich reddish purple); 'Compacta' (semidwarf form, 3' × 3'); 'Orange Flame' (new growth bronze orange; wine-red winter foliage) **SIZE/HABIT:** 6' × 5', upright (shorter in full sun)

BOTANICAL NAME: *M. wagneri* (hybrid of *M. aquifolium* and *M. pinnata*) **CULTIVARS/COMMENTS:** 'Pinnacle' (vigorous and erect; rich yellow flowers);'Undulata' (spiny leaflets have wavy margins) **SIZE/HABIT:** 8' × 5', upright **GROUNDCOVERS:** Tough, hardy, low-growing, drought-tolerant species that spread freely by underground runners. Flowers and berries are in scale with their size. Best used for massed planting, groundcover, erosion control, hillside plantings, native gardens, naturalizing and as food and cover for birds and wildlife. May be slow to establish, but will eventually make dense patches.

BOTANICAL/COMMON NAME: *M. nervosa* (longleaf mahonia) **CULTIVARS/COMMENTS:** Best in partial shade (good woodlander); shorter, redder, and slower growing in full sun; needs acidic soil **SIZE/HABIT:** 18" to 24" tall, suckering

BOTANICAL NAME: *M. repens* (creeping mahonia) **CULTIVARS/COMMENTS:** Shorter in full sun; resembles compact *M. aquifolium* and is similarly adaptable; sun or shade; 'Rotundifolia' is tall form with rounded, almost spineless leaves. **SIZE/HABIT:** 24" to 36" tall, suckering

A FANCY FOR FUCHSIAS

by WAYNE WINTERROWD

Born in 1501, Leonhart Fuchs would have had no opportunity to examine a dried specimen, or even a drawing, of any of the more than 100 species in the genus that bears his name.

They, denizens of the New World from Mexico to Patagonia (with three isolated species in New Zealand and Tahiti), inhabited lands then largely unguessed at. And he — in a life of 66 years that passed for long at that time — was busy translating Galen and Hippocrates into Latin, curing many of the "English Sweating Sicknesses" in the duchy of Anspach, and finally, until his death, occupying the professorship of medicine at the University of Tübingen. For all these distinctions, he would merit only a short paragraph in any modern encyclopedia.

But for two others, he deserves a bow from gardeners living now, almost 500 years later. In 1542 he published a work of botany (his passionate hobby) entitled *De historia stirpium commentarii insignes,* in which he described for the first time the common foxglove and attached to its genus forever the name *Digitalis.* And in 1703 the French botanist Plumier chose to honor Fuchs by affixing his name (in *Nova plantarum Americanum genera*) to his description of the plant we now know as *Fuchsia triphylla.* Thus, Leonhart Fuchs became associated with a genus of familiar garden plants he could never have seen — fuchsias were not brought into cultivation in Europe until 1788 — and with thousands of hybrids he certainly could never even have dreamed of.

Most of those hybrids are complex crosses, principally of *F. fulgens* and *F. magellanica* (and their progeny), with the result that most florists' fuchsias can have no more-accurate designation than

Fuchsia arborescens

F. hybrida, the botanist's way of throwing up his hands in nomenclatural despair. Within the estimated 3,000 to 5,000 cultivars of *F. hybrida,* one can have almost anything. There are plants that are stubbornly upright in growth, gracefully arching or vinelike. Leaves may be as big and dark as a privet's or almost as tiny and pale as chickweed, some veined in purple and many splashed or margined with cream or white. Flowers may be as large as a wine cork or smaller than a pencil eraser, slim or chubby, with upturned or down-hanging sepals and tightly cupped or flared corollas. These corollas may be sublimely single with only four petals; semidouble, with eight or double, with heaven knows how many. Flower color can be anything but

---

general **CULTURE**

All fuchsias crave cool, buoyant air that is high in moisture. In the privileged places where such conditions conjoin with the absence of heavy frost (such as northern California and the Pacific Northwest), they are superb garden shrubs, living happily in the ground and increasing in beauty over many years. In most American gardens, however, they are summer pot plants of brief or extended lives, depending on how closely their needs for atmospheric comfort can be met. Though in latitudes as far north as Vermont they may be grown in full sun, farther south they are happiest in the place you like to sit on a sunny summer day — a breezy porch or under the high shade of trees. If, however, the place you like to sit on such days is indoors, with the air conditioning at full blast, then fuchsias will sulk horribly by midsummer and must essentially be treated as transitory, early-summer decoration.

Fuchsia 'Gartenmeister Bonstedt'

Fuchsia magellanica

the primary colors, but some hybrids inch so close to orange or crimson or deep, bluish purple as almost to be there. And because a fuchsia "flower" has two distinct parts, the sepal and the corolla, each can be separately colored to make practically infinite combinations. Like the modern bearded iris and the daylily, *F. hybrida* is therefore a breeder's or a collector's dream (or perhaps nightmare).

The Best Hybrid Fuchsia

Among so many possibilities, selecting the one best fuchsia might seem difficult as Galahad's quest for the Holy Grail. Actually, it is not so, for all who love fuchsias take off their hats before *F.* 'Hidcote Beauty'. Its creator is unknown, though it was bred about 1949 and was treasured by Lawrence Johnston, who grew it in his garden at Hidcote and named it. Its blossoms are as far from the modern doubled hybrids as can be, consisting of sepals so pale a pink as almost to be white but tinged at their tips with lime-green shadows and a corolla of that indescribable color only else seen in precious seashells. Blossoms are relatively small — hardly 1.5" long — but they are so numerous that a healthy plant seems to drip with them. Though generally one starts one's love affair with fuchsias with a casual purchase in early summer of a healthy, pretty plant if the love continues, one will end up, sooner or later, with 'Hidcote Beauty'. Or at least, one should.

As it happens, hybrid fuchsias such as 'Hidcote Beauty' are, among all tender shrubs, perhaps the easiest and the most satisfying to train as standards. As small trees they display their dangling flowers with far more suaveness than when suspended in a plastic pot from the porch eaves. With careful winter management they may eventually achieve full heads of flower and trunks as thick as a shovel handle. Wherever they are stood, they convey at once a sense of sophistication and the cottager's love of a good plant and his at-

propagation

Rooting any fuchsia is ease itself, provided cuttings are taken at the right time. The ideal consists of the first, vigorous late-spring growth of the plant, when shoots are elongating and flower buds first appearing. About 6" is just right, severing the cutting below two fully formed leaves where soft, lettucey tissue makes its transition to a mature, darker-colored stem. The lower pair (or perhaps two pairs) of leaves should be stripped away, along with all flower buds, and the cutting inserted in half peat, half sharp sand and kept moist and shaded until fresh growth shows that roots have formed. It can then be potted in an ordinary potting mix and pinched at the top to begin the formation of a well-balanced plant. Cuttings taken at other times are still worth a try, for a little more coddling, a dip perhaps in mild rooting hormone, a plastic bag and a spritz of water can still mean success.

At summer's end, a thriving potted specimen naturally brings up the challenge of saving it for another season of beauty. This is relatively easy to do. By late August a fuchsia will indicate that it has completed its natural cycle of growth by slowing down the production of new shoots and flowers. Because fuchsias bloom on new growth and resprout freely from old wood, the plant should be cut back hard before it has experienced frost, leaving only a scaffold of bare branches. It should then be brought under frost-free cover and kept moderately dry to trigger complete dormancy. Winter conditions should be as cool as possible, ideally hovering between 40°F and 55°F. Only enough water should be supplied to keep the roots alive and the wood from shriveling.

Somewhere around early March, new growth buds will appear, indicating that the plant is ready to resume growth. At that time, it should be shaken from its pot and as much old compost as possible teased from around its root ball with a chopstick or pencil. Dangling roots should be clipped away by about a third, and the plant repotted in fresh potting mix, whether in its original pot or in one just slightly larger. Watering should remain cautious until the new shoots begin to expand vigorously, at which point the plant will need bright but still cool conditions, though it should be protected from the full force of the early spring sun, which will scorch emerging leaves. Each new shoot should be pinched after it has produced two full sets of leaves, and the resulting shoots pinched again, to build up a rich, full head of growth. Pinching should cease about four weeks before the last frost-free date, after which the plant may be safely moved outdoors. Still, the weather must be carefully watched, because when in fresh spring growth, hybrid fuchsias are severely damaged or even killed outright at temperatures much below 40°F.

tention to its management. They thus represent that marriage between formality and exuberance of flower that was pioneered by Lawrence Johnston at Hidcote, and which has been for the last 50 years the most fruitful of garden styles throughout the world. It is perhaps no accident, then, that 'Hidcote Beauty' makes the very best standard.

Species Fuchsias

When any plant has proven itself willing to be extensively hybridized, discriminating gardeners become curious about the true species and want them also. In their simplicity they seem always to carry a sense of innocence and directness that further charms a heart already won. Gardeners who are lucky enough to live in the cool, fog-drenched and frost-free sections of the American Northwest can collect them all, for they will thrive there like any forsythia elsewhere, making, in many cases, sturdy hedges and barrier screens or single specimens of arresting beauty. For the rest of us, an occasional species fuchsia as a summer-blooming pot plant or a few more if we are lucky enough to have a cool greenhouse or heated sunporch, will have to serve.

Choices among species fuchsias range above a hundred. Within that number are many treasures, such as *F. boliviana*, which can grow to 20', but can be hard-pruned to make an attractive large pot plant or tubbed conservatory shrub. It flowers profusely throughout the bright months, producing down-hanging panicles of many narrow, tubular 2" blossoms of deep, vibrant pink. The variety *alba* is particularly choice with white sepals and a flared red corolla, all

hybrid fuchsias

The popular cultivars pictured below give an idea of the range of shapes and colors that are currently available.

Fuchsia 'Angel's Dream'

Fuchsia 'Swingtime'

Fuchsia 'Indian Maid'

Fuchsia 'Pink Galore'

Fuchsia 'Mrs. Marshall'

Fuchsia 'Mary'

Fuchsia 'Hidcote Beauty'

Valentine-colored in effect. *Fuchsia arborescens* can, as its name implies, assume stout, treelike proportions to 30', and so for pot culture is best repropagated from cuttings every three or four years. Fortunately, it blooms while quite young, producing thick panicles of bloom in luminous pink.

Of all species fuchsias, the easiest to acquire possesses also the greatest historical interest, for it is *F. triphylla* that was first described by Plumier in 1703, and, many years later, the first of the genus ever cultivated in Europe. In the form of its hybrid offspring, 'Gartenmeister Bonstedt', it appears with fair regularity in nurseries and mail-order catalogs. Of sturdy, upright growth to 3', it makes a handsome, tidy shrub, clad in dark green leaves veined with bur-

gundy. Each growing stem is terminated by a panicle of scarlet tubes about 2" long at maturity. The sepals clasp the corolla tightly, so the effect is of a slender, unified flower rather than the two-part "lady's eardrop." Nicely, even the tiniest buds at the center of the panicle color, so the effect is of a thick bunch of scarlet tubes hanging all together in the manner of honeysuckles, from which it takes its common name, the honeysuckle fuchsia.

But the greatest excitement among gardeners has been occasioned by the many forms of *F. magellanica* that have recently become available. The species occurs in many variations across its extensive range in Argentina and southern Chile. It forms a lax, mounded shrub that may sometimes build up to 8', with slender red-tinted stems and narrow, .5"- to 1"-long leaves. Though typically a fresh green, those leaves may veer to gold or be splashed with silver. A healthy plant seems always to be abundantly furnished with flowers, which are tiny but hang gracefully from stems 1" or more long. The color of the sepals is typically a rich red and the corolla is purple, though cultivars have been selected that are all white or white flushed with pale pink, or with contrasting parts in deeper or paler reds or purples. In all forms the stamens and stigma extend $\frac{1}{2}$" beyond the corolla and are also richly colored, adding to the delicate charm of each blossom. In the ground or in a pot, cultivars of *F. magellanica* are surprisingly unfussy, tolerating a lapse in watering without throwing disfiguring tantrums. Where they are hardy, they make superb hedges.

The great question is, Where, exactly, are they hardy? Certainly in the milder parts of northern California and the Northwest, where, though they may occasionally be killed to the ground, they quickly regrow. But because of its natural range, *F. magellanica* seemed to hold the promise of being able to endure significant cold, at least if properly mounded up and covered with straw or evergreen boughs. The cultivar 'Riccartonii', once given its own specific standing, was said to be especially cold-tolerant, though Hortus III ambiguously remarks that it is "relatively very hardy." Enough in that for a try, and many eastern gardeners have. Some have succeeded in bringing plants through the winter, at least once. Most have failed. But treated like any other fuchsia, which is to say as a tender shrub, *F. magellanica* is still a charming plant. Because of its dainty flowers and its quick, shrubby growth, it may be slipped from its pot to fill a gap in the perennial border, without ever looking anomalous and "floristy."

growing FUCHSIAS IN POTS

As with African violets, the cultural requirements of fuchsias are simple but strict. The first is a fibrous and moisture-retentive soil that is also very free draining. An adequate mix can be made by combining equal parts good garden loam, crumbly leaf mold and well-rotted cow manure, with a sprinkling of sharp sand or perlite. Much easier (lacking the cow) is a good, peat-based, soilless potting mix such as Pro-Mix. More than usual care should be taken in placing bits of broken crockery in the bottom of the pot, as perfect drainage is an absolute requirement of all fuchsias.

Where drainage is perfect, one can almost never overwater a fuchsia, and plants also benefit hugely from frequent wetting of the foliage, which raises atmospheric humidity and mimics their cool, high-mountain homelands. Like many plants that crave moisture, fuchsias are also greedy feeders and nourishment is best supplied by a water-soluble plant food, at half the strength recommended on the package but twice as often, or (assuming the cow) by frequent doses of weak manure tea. Some growers report great success with soluble fertilizer specially fabricated for tomatoes. When well potted and well nourished, a fuchsia will respond almost before one's eyes with vigorous, healthy growth; rich, abundant leaves and flowers produced from every leaf axil from late May to September.

MOUNTAIN LAUREL RENAISSANCE

by RICHARD A. JAYNES

Mountain laurel, *Kalmia latifolia*, has been called, with some justification,
America's most beautiful flowering shrub.

The clusters of light pink, architecturally perfect flowers appear in late spring on spreading, many-branched shrubs bearing glossy, evergreen leaves. It is an eastern plant, found on well-drained acid soils from Maine to the Gulf Coast and is especially common in the uplands within that range. Connecticut and Pennsylvania both claim this beautiful shrub as their state flower. Plants in the southern Appalachians have been known to reach 35' in height; plants in cultivation, however, are generally considered mature at 10' to 15'.

Like its close relatives the rhododendrons, mountain laurel has been grown as a garden plant for over 200 years. Most plants sold now are nursery grown, but collection from native stands still occurs and used to be common practice. The best plants were ob-tained two or three years after an area had been clear-cut. With the trees removed, laurels that had been cut to the ground would re-sprout and develop into dense, multistemmed plants.

Foresters do not necessarily view mountain laurel with the same affection as gardeners. Laurel thickets, also colorfully called "laurel hells," can be so dense that they prevent the regeneration of hard-wood trees, and the tangle of stems can be almost impossible to walk through. Such thickets, of course, provide great cover for birds, deer and other animals.

Until recently there was a widespread belief that there is just one standard kind of mountain laurel flower — light pink in bud and near white when open. But botanical and horticultural journals

indicate that by the late 1800s several unusual flower and foliage forms had been discovered. By the mid-1900s, C. O. Dexter and other plantsmen had been selecting seed from the best wild pink-flowering laurels, as well as from their offspring, and in successive generations they began to select seedlings whose flowers were not only a rich, vibrant pink, but some that were also red in bud.

In 1961 I had just received my Ph.D. doing research on chestnuts and, as a new employee at the Connecticut Agricultural Experiment Station, was looking for another plant to study. Mountain laurels caught my attention, for a number of reasons: the genus was manageable, with only seven species; mountain laurel was the state flower; it was a beautiful and desirable shrub in both the wild and cultivated landscapes; and little horticultural research had been done on the genus. As I read the literature and talked with plants-people, the potential of *Kalmia* began to unfold. Over the last 25 years a number of us have been able to breed and select a range of new cultivars using unusual traits found in nature, for example, plants of small stature with small leaves; willow-shaped leaves; and a color range from pure white to near red, as well as other variations. For me, the most distinctive of the new cultivars are the littleleaf or miniature laurels, derived from a rare native form of *K. latifolia* called *myrtifolia* for its myrtle-like leaves. Five littleleaf cultivars have been named so far: 'Elf', near white in flower; 'Minuet', which has a cinnamon-maroon band on the inside of the flower; 'Tiddlywinks' and 'Tinkerbell', both pink; and 'Little Linda', which is red in bud. Though all have small leaves, the flowers are relatively large, and growth is one-half to two-thirds that of regular laurels, except for 'Tinkerbell', which is as vigorous as the larger-leaved laurels.

Three unique laurels that might become available in the future deserve mention. 'Tightwad Too' was found in a native stand in Wilton, Connecticut. It buds up one or two weeks later than other mountain laurels, at which point the flowers look like they will open in a couple of days, but they never do. These unopened buds remain attractive up to a month longer than the flowers of regular mountain laurels. 'Madeline' is a double-flowered laurel with rich pink buds. The original plant — the only double form ever found — came from New Zealand, having apparently arrived there as an unflowered seedling from Massachusetts. 'Creepy' was found growing in Wahalla, South Carolina. It is no more than 18" high but approximately 20' across, and has the potential to be a great groundcover. Who knows how many more unique and useful forms of mountain laurel there are to be found in gardens or in the thousands of acres of native laurels?

Although mountain laurel seems to grow in all sorts of conditions in the wild, it can be finicky in the garden. As in nature, acid, well-drained soils are best. Very rich, wet, compacted or clay soils are not likely to give good results. Marginal soils can be improved by incorporating large amounts of coarse organic material, such as aged pine bark. With heavy soils, it is advisable to raise the planting bed several inches above the surrounding soil. Organic mulches are also a good idea, as are light applications of fertilizer for acid-loving plants. Although mountain laurel is found in woodlands and is shade tolerant, blooming will be heavier and foliage more dense in openings or on the edge of the woods in at least dappled sunlight.

Because mountain laurel has such an extensive natural range, it is difficult to give hard-and-fast information about hardiness. Though wild plants from the southern part of the range may closely resemble those from the northern part, they do not harden off and overwinter well in the north. The hardiness of cultivars can also be variable, depending upon where they were selected. Most of the cultivars raised in Connecticut and Massachusetts are hardy to USDA Zone 5. Some are even hardy to Zone 4, but more experience is needed.

Few serious insect and disease problems regularly afflict mountain laurel, except possibly leafspot, a foliage disease caused by a fungus. Plants in heavy shade are the most susceptible, whereas plants grown in sun, or where foliage does not remain covered with moisture for long periods of time, are seldom affected.

Search out some of the new mountain laurels. Not all plant outlets have them, but once in your garden they will be highly prized.

LATE-BLOOMING EUCRYPHIA ×NYMANSENSIS

by THOMAS FISCHER

First impressions are lasting, which is why I remember the first time I saw a eucryphia in bloom. It was the beginning of September — not the most common time of year for a tree to be covered with large, white flowers — at, appropriately enough, Mount Usher Gardens in County Wicklow, Ireland. This was where 'Mount Usher' was raised in the 1920s, one of two cultivars of *Eucryphia ×nymansensis,* itself a cross between two South American species, *E. cordifolia* and *E. glutinosa.* The other cultivar, 'Nymansay' — the more common of the two — was the result of a cross in 1914 at Nymans, Sussex.

In the United States, *E. ×nymansensis* is hardy only in the cool, maritime climates of the West. Even there, a sudden harsh turn of winter weather can kill off the top or burn the leaves, but the tree

usually recovers well. The plant has a narrow, columnar form and grows to about 30' high. Eucryphias prefer part to full sun with their roots in the shade. A good organic mulch will help retain moisture in our dry northwestern summers.

The foliage has a pleasingly crisp look to it. The leaves — simple or sometimes compound with three leaflets — are dark, glossy green, coarsely serrated and slightly undulate (with a wavy margin). The branches grow in an upswept fashion, giving the tree a formal appearance. But it's the August and September flower show that grabs you. The flowers, which appear singly in the leaf axils, are slightly cup shaped, white and 2.5" wide, with a mass of terra-cotta-colored anthers in the middle. They release a light honey scent, and attract an untold number of bees. Mostly four-petaled, the flowers of 'Mount Usher' are sometimes double.

In the garden of a friend of mine, *E. ×nymansensis* figures prominently in a snappy, green-and-white, east-facing entryway planting, in which the Mexican orange (*Choisya ternata*) and the low-growing *Rhododendron* 'Lucy Lou' cluster around the eucryphia's base. For a more colorful combination, you could surround the eucryphia with a group of Pacific Northwest natives such as the red flowering currant (*Ribes sanguineum*), yellow-flowered, low-growing Oregon grape (*Mahonia nervosa*) or pink-flowered Nootka rose (*Rosa nutkana*). My recently planted 'Nymansay' shares space with a planting of variegated moor grass (*Molinia caerulea* subsp. *caerulea* 'Variegata'). The beach strawberry (*Fragaria chiloensis*), native to the west coasts of both North and South America, is hopping its way over to become a glossy green groundcover around the eucryphia, thereby connecting our two continents.

at a GLANCE

TYPE OF PLANT: small evergreen tree **FAMILY:** Eucryphiaceae (eucryphia family) **HEIGHT:** 30' to 50' **HABIT:** narrow, stiffly upright; single, occasionally multi-trunked **LEAVES:** simple or compound with three leaflets; glossy, dark green above; sharply serrate; 1.5" to 3" long **FLOWERS:** solitary, pure white with overlapping petals and yellow anthers; to 2.5" across **BARK:** smooth and gray **RATE OF GROWTH:** medium **HARDINESS:** USDA Zones 7–9 **EXPOSURE:** full sun or part shade; shaded root zone; protect from harsh wind **SOIL:** well drained, neutral to slightly acid **WATER NEEDS:** regular **FEEDING:** not necessary **PROPAGATION:** by semiripe cuttings **PROBLEMS:** winter dieback possible

SHOWY SKIMMIA JAPONICA

by THOMAS FISCHER

Gardeners, I may say from personal experience, are no less prone to idiotic ideas than the rest of the populace. Wouldn't it be grand, I thought recently, to have a Japanese woodland in the front yard? The fact that Boston is not Japan, and that the front yard is already pretty well planted up, did not obtrude into this process. Ultimately, faced with the grim realities of limited space and increasingly skittish neighbors, the plans for bamboo groves and copses of Japanese maples had to be given up. But not, I am happy to report, the skimmias, of which there are now eight lining a path on either side in charming fashion, like a family of green turtles. It is not a Japanese woodland, but it is enough. For now.

Skimmia japonica is the species you are most likely to find in nurseries and mail-order catalogs, and since it is as beautiful as any other member of the genus, there is no need to go whoring after novelties. Each shrub forms a neat, domelike mound of dark green, glossy foliage that grows slowly to about 3' to 4' high and as much across. The essential fact to bear in mind is that the species is dioecious — that is, male and female flowers are borne on separate plants. Thus, if you want to get a late-fall or winter crop of the conspicuous red fruits — and you assuredly do — then you will need at least one male plant to pollinate your females. Actually, the male plants would be worth having even if they weren't needed for stud duty, because their flower clusters, which begin forming in the fall, are even showier than those of the females, with deep red buds that open in early spring to small white flowers. They also carry the bonus of a delicious fragrance, which is almost undetectable in the females. If you can bring yourself to sacrifice a few branches, both the female berry clusters and the male flower buds, taken with some of the foliage, make excellent evergreenery for decorating the house during the holidays. (In fact, I've begun to see the male flowers turning up at some of the tonier florist shops around town.)

Though I wouldn't characterize *S. japonica* as fussy, it does need shade (sun scorches the foliage), which can be quite deep, provided the site in which the shrubs are planted isn't inordinately dry and rooty. The soil should also be on the acid side of neutral (below pH

7.0), and supplemental water may be needed during dry spells. A mulch of shredded oak leaves or pine straw is a good idea, in any event. Also, the hotter and muggier the climate, the more susceptible *S. japonica* becomes to spider mite damage, which means that it's not a good choice for the lower South. OK, so maybe it *is* a little fussy. However, if you can provide the conditions it needs, I'd be surprised if this trim, elegant woodlander didn't quickly rise to the top of your list of favorites.

at a GLANCE

TYPE OF PLANT: evergreen shrub **FAMILY:** Rutaceae **HEIGHT/SPREAD:** both 3' to 4' (exceptionally to 6') **HABIT:** mounded, domelike **LEAVES:** elliptic-oblong, simple, dark glossy green above, yellow green beneath, 2" to 5" long **FLOWERS:** .33" across, creamy white, opening from reddish-maroon buds, borne in panicles 2" long and wide; male flowers are larger and more fragrant **BLOOM PERIOD:** March–April **FRUITS:** bright red, .33" across, ripening in October and held through winter, borne only on female plants **HARDINESS:** USDA Zones 6–9 **PROPAGATION:** by seed (cleaned of pulp) or cuttings taken in fall and treated with rooting hormone **PROBLEMS:** none serious; occasionally, foliage may be disfigured by mites

RADIANT JAPANESE SPICEBUSH

by THOMAS FISCHER

If you have a predominantly shady garden, there are two courses of action you can adopt.

One is to sit around feeling sorry for yourself because you can't grow good roses. The other is to get busy and find out what plants will both thrive in the conditions you can provide and at the same time help lighten the gloom. While there's no shortage of gloom-dispersing plants in the herbaceous realm, the pickings get leaner when it comes to shrubs and especially shrubs with emphatic, eye-catching foliage. There are a few, however. One of my favorites is *Lindera obtusiloba,* even though it waits until the fall to crank up the wattage. Not that it's too shabby earlier in the season. From late spring through summer's end this rounded, large-growing native of Japan, China and Korea is clothed with lustrous, 4" to 6", dark green leaves that may be unlobed, three-lobed, or two-lobed, like a mitten. (This variety of leaf shapes may remind you of sassafras, which belongs to the same family, the Lauraceae.) Then, in October the show begins. From top to bottom, Japanese spicebush turns a brilliant yellow, even in the shade,

and holds its color for a good two to three weeks. If you have enough room for both a male and female specimen, you'll also get a crop of handsome red fruits that eventually turn a glossy black.

Even though my own plant grows in the shade of a large red oak, Japanese spicebush is also perfectly happy in full sun and isn't particular about soil type. Although a constant, moderate level of moisture is ideal (especially when a young plant is settling in), established shrubs will put up with both occasional dry spells and periods of wetness, provided drainage is good.

As much as I look forward to its annual display of fireworks, I also value it for the contrast its bold foliage offers in my garden to its fine-leaved neighbors and for the way it serves as a visual anchor for the sea of hellebores that swirls around its base. Considered individually, Japanese spicebush's virtues may seem modest, but they add up to a shrub of the first rank.

---

at a GLANCE

TYPE OF PLANT: deciduous shrub **FAMILY:** Lauraceae **HEIGHT:** 10' to 12' **HABIT:** rounded, multistemmed **LEAVES:** ovate, cordate at base, entire to three-lobed, 4" to 6" long, conspicuously three-veined, deep green turning brilliant yellow in fall. **FLOWERS:** small, greenish yellow, not very showy, borne in early spring **FRUITS:** .25" in diameter, red turning to black, borne only on female plants **HARDINESS:** USDA Zones 6–10 **PROPAGATION:** by softwood cuttings in midsummer or seed given a three-month cold stratification period **PROBLEMS:** None serious.

IN PRAISE OF RHODODENDRON 'KEN JANECK'

by RICHARD BROOKS

Few landscape shrubs are as highly valued for today's gardens as rhododendrons.

Their lush evergreen foliage, exuberant floral display and permanence have earned them the highest ratings among home gardeners and landscape professionals alike. Yet the kinds commonly offered and widely planted too often outgrow the locations assigned to them, becoming leggy, awkward and sprawling with age.

Good news! Among the thousand species and countless hybrids in this vast and diverse genus, there are many with a more restrained and compact habit of growth. *Rhododendron yakushimanum* (now properly *R. degronianum* subsp. *yakushimanum*) and its hybrids, dubbed "yaks" by aficionados, are good examples. And among the yaks, the cultivar 'Ken Janeck' stands out as a nearly perfect broad-leaved evergreen. 'Ken Janeck' forms a rounded mound of densely branching habit, 3' tall and as wide in 10 years in a sunny location, and somewhat taller and wider in shade.

Its luxuriant foliage emerges in late spring, clad in a fuzzy white coating that contrasts handsomely with the older, glossy, dark green

leaves. Gradually during the summer this coating washes off the upper surface of the leaves, but the leaf underside retains a thick, feltlike covering (technically known as indumentum) that matures to an attractive beige color. I like to invite visitors to the garden to stroke a leaf and then turn it over to admire this palpable bit of nature's handiwork. It seems that this attractive feature has a practical purpose, too, for insect pests rarely attack the leaves. Imagine yourself a caterpillar, finding that you had bitten off a mouthful of cotton flannel instead of a succulent salad!

With every desirable attribute as a year-round shrub in the landscape, 'Ken Janeck' also produces beautiful flowers — a true bonus. Reddish pink buds open to soft pink flowers that mature to white over several days; a plant covered in bloom at the half-open stage gives a delightful effect, reminiscent of freshly opened apple blossoms. Bloom time varies depending on location; in the Pacific Northwest it can occur in April, but here in my New England garden, I look forward to peak bloom at the end of May.

Rhododendron yakushimanum and its various named selections are listed as bud-hardy to –15°F or –25°F by various authorities, a perplexing spread. However, in the 20-some years that 'Ken Janeck' has inhabited my USDA Zone 5 garden, it has never failed to bloom, and we have had winter lows in the –15°F to –20°F range in that time.

Cultural requirements are as for any rhododendron: acid, well-drained soil, well fortified with copious amounts of organic matter, shallow planting (don't cover the root ball) and a year-round mulch of chopped leaves, pine needles, bark or the equivalent. In the Pacific Northwest and similar cool-summer climates, 'Ken Janeck' will thrive in full sun, but in the warmer East, and especially in the South, some shade is beneficial — either dappled shade all day, or a half-day of sun and half-day of shade.

Among rhododendron enthusiasts there is spirited debate as to whether 'Ken Janeck' is a selected form of the species *R. yakushimanum* or a hybrid between *R. yakushimanum* and another species, presumably *R. smirnowii*. Those conflicting opinions alter not one whit the tremendous contribution that this fine plant can make to any landscape. And in confirmation of its outstanding qualities, 'Ken Janeck' was granted the coveted Award of Excellence by the American Rhododendron Society.

SPRING INTO SNOWDROPS

by CAROL KLEIN

During the bleak winter months, when we can no longer pursue our favorite pastime, depression becomes rife.

You can spend only so long comfortably ensconced in an armchair perusing nursery catalogs and ordering next year's seeds before being overwhelmed by the desire to see and touch real plants. Snowdrops offer salvation. To discover a plant that is at its peak when all else is dormant (and in many cases totally subterranean) is an uplifting experience. And because of the cyclical nature of gardening, it is one that we can look forward to every year — a firm reassurance that spring is on the way.

Who doesn't love snowdrops? The sight of their gray-green shoots pushing through the sleeping earth is all it takes to banish dejection. The swordlike leaves pierce the soil, each one curiously swollen in its middle, pregnant with its precious bud. The stems lengthen, divide and launch the flower, which is upright at first then gently leaning until it acquires its typical bell-like shape, suspended on an arching, hair-thin stem. As the days go by, new flowers emerge and each flower swells so that the area of white within a planting increases steadily.

Some Favorites

Galanthus nivalis is the first choice for a wild, woodland planting. In Great Britain, it is this species that adorns our woods and ditches. Although our climate is mild, *G. nivalis* is hardy to USDA Zone 3, as are many of the other most popular species and varieties. Populations grow by bulbs dividing spontaneously, and by seed. As the flowers fade the stems lengthen, the ovary fattens and is brought down by its own increased weight until it is level with the earth. In this way, year on year, colonies increase and expand. Although the double variety, *Galanthus*

Galanthus 'Atkinsii'

TYPE OF PLANT: hardy bulb **FAMILY:** Amaryllidaceae (amaryllis family) **ORIGINS:** western Europe to Iranian Caucasus and Caspian Sea **HARDINESS:** USDA Zones 3–9 (most species) **HEIGHT:** 4" to 12" **LEAVES:** paired, strap shaped, narrow to broad, bright green to glaucous **FLOWERS:** solitary, borne on short pedicel, with six unequal perianth segments; outer segments longer, pure white; inner segments much shorter, marked green; usually nodding **BLOOM PERIOD:** midwinter–early spring, depending on climate and variety **SOIL:** somewhat heavy, humus-rich, moisture retentive, well drained **Exposure:** partial shade (most varieties); *G. elwesii* and *G. gracilis* will grow in full sun **WATERING:** plentiful moisture needed during growth period in winter and spring; some dryness tolerated in summer **PLANTING TIME:** early fall **FEEDING:** annual mulch of leaf mold or compost **PROPAGATION:** by division immediately after flowering **PROBLEMS:** none serious

nivalis f. *pleniflorus* 'Flore Pleno', increases fast and is exquisite with its multilayered white petticoats edged in green, it lacks the simple elegance of the single form.

There are other appealing snowdrops that are both easy to cultivate and increase well. *Galanthus* 'Atkinsii' is a large, robust snowdrop with long flared petals. Where I garden in Devon (the equivalent of a warm USDA Zone 8), it appears early in the year, often during January and sometimes through snow. Although it will colonize quickly of its own volition, if you have a plan for it you can dig it up as it fades, knock the soil from the bulbs, and replant them separately a few inches apart and 4" to 6" deep. Give each bulb a ration of good, humusy compost, preferably mixed with leaf mold. (This is a prescription that suits all snowdrops.) Vary the distances between the bulbs to ensure a random, natural look. Within a short space of time, big drifts can result. Sue Staines, who gardens with her husband Wal at Glenn Chantry (where the photographs for this chapter were taken), has what she describes as a "river of white" that runs from the house to the front gate, composed entirely of *G.* 'Atkinsii'. Sue's advice to anyone who is starting a collection is to plant one of the easier and more prolific varieties first to see how well it will do in the conditions their garden has to offer before investing large sums for rarer varieties. (And some of the choicer

varieties can command as much as £40/$60 per bulb.) This is not a question of having to make do with second best, however — quite a number of the classic varieties are not prohibitively expensive and will multiply rapidly.

One of these easy classics is *G.* 'S. Arnott', which blooms a little later than *G.* 'Atkinsii', opening its perfect rounded flowers in February. It is a *G. nivalis* seedling, and as such loves heavy damp soils, in which it will increase rapidly. It was developed by the famous Walter Butt, who planted it in his garden at Chalford in Gloucestershire. Later in its life the garden was bought by Brigadier and Mrs. Mathias, who eventually founded the Giant Snowdrop Company. Not only did they make available to the public the snowdrops from the garden which had increased into enormous clumps over the years, but they also collected and increased every good snowdrop they could find. It is thanks to them that many old and rare varieties were propagated and shared.

Galanthus 'Magnet' is another variety recommended for beginners, although it is equally popular with the snowdrop cognoscenti. It is a strong grower of medium height with a very long pedicel that allows the flower to move around gracefully in the breeze. It may look fragile, but its looks belie its incredible tenacity.

How and Where to Grow Snowdrops

There are snowdrops to suit a wide range of cultural and climatic conditions. *Galanthus nivalis* varieties, which constitute the majority of cultivated snowdrops, luxuriate in damp winter conditions but prefer to be drier during the summer. A site in heavy soil among the roots of deciduous trees suits them perfectly. Not everyone has the luxury of space for a separate spring woodland garden, but even one tree can provide a perfect environment for clumps of snowdrops planted through drifts of later-blooming shade-lovers. You don't even need a tree —

Next page: 1. *Galanthus* 'S. Arnott'. Perfect rounded petals. 6". Increases well. **2.** *Galanthus nivalis* f. *pleniflorus* 'Blewbury Tart'. Its upward-facing flowers are unlike any other snowdrop. Charming. **3.** *Galanthus nivalis* 'Viridapice'. A striking, easily grown snowdrop that has strong solid green markings on the outer segments. **4.** *Galanthus* 'Atkinsii'. An old cultivar with an established pedigree as a garden plant. **5.** *Galanthus nivalis* f. *pleniflorus* 'Walrus'. According to snowdrop expert Matt Bishop, "one of the great eccentrics of the snowdrop world." **6.** *Galanthus* 'John Gray'. A classic — one of the biggest of all snowdrops. Poised and elegant. **7.** *Galanthus plicatus* 'Trym'. A cult hybrid whose outer petals form a "Chinese pagoda" around the inner petals. **8.** *Galanthus* 'Jacquenetta'. Neat and very double. One of the *Greatorex* doubles, all very similar to the untrained eye. **9.** *Galanthus nivalis* 'Sandersii'. The ovary, inner markings and pedicel are all yellow. Found originally in Northumberland, England.

Sue Staines, for example, grows many of her special snowdrops in the middle of broad island beds among big clumps of perennials. In the winter, when the herbaceous plants are absent, the snowdrops can be viewed clearly. Then, in the summer, the perennials lend cool shelter to the now dormant snowdrops. A good moisture-retaining mulch is helpful in this kind of situation.

Some snowdrops are from much warmer climes and are happy in a sunny site. One of the first snowdrops to flower, *G. elwesii* has broad, glaucous leaves that clasp the flower stem and inner petals marked with green. Although it comes from Turkey, it is perfectly tough and will stand winter temperatures as low as −15°F (USDA Zone 5a). *Galanthus elwesii* Edward Whittall Group is one of its best forms, with especially green underskirts. Also happy in sun is *G. gracilis* (formerly *G. graecus*), a small snowdrop with characteristically twisted leaves.

Snowdrop Memories

Looking at the great variety to be found among snowdrops, it's easy to understand how they can become a passion in adult life. The roots of my involvement with them go much deeper, however. One of the abiding memories of my childhood was the arrival of a cardboard box each January at my grandmother's home from one of her sisters in Cornwall. My grandmother would delay opening the parcel until she could corral any spare grandchildren into the glass porch where the parcel sat smothered in stamps, string and sealing wax. Off came the lid of the box, revealing a further bundle, this time of soft green moss. It was gently but eagerly peeled away to reveal a big bunch of pristine snowdrops. A small jug full of water was already standing by to receive the precious flowers, and later, when they had had a chance to recover, we were each given a few to take home. I can remember their honeyed scent exactly and the delicate green lines traced around their inner petals.

Everyone must grow snowdrops.

design TIPS

Opinions vary about how to associate snowdrops with other plants, but most gardeners agree they do not lend themselves to formal schemes — straight lines are definitely out — and that they should be planted en masse. Here are some suggestions for successful combinations.

• More vigorous varieties can hold their own in naturalistic plantings with grassy subjects like *Carex comans* or *Stipa tenuissima* planted around shrubs like the red-stemmed *Cornus alba* or the fiery, twiggy *Cornus sanguinea* 'Midwinter Fire'.

• The pristine whiteness of all snowdrops makes a telling contrast to any dark-leaved plant. The usual favorite is black mondo grass, *Ophiopogon planiscapus* 'Nigrescens', but this has been somewhat overdone. Try one of the double snowdrops with the near-black, palmate leaves of *Geranium pratense* 'Purple-haze', which should be coming into growth at about the same time as the first snowdrops open. Alternatively, the patterned foliage of heuchera varieties would provide good contrasting hummocks of purple and crimson.

• One of the most attractive snowdrop associations in our garden is with our darkest hellebores, which have plum-colored foliage. As an undercover, *Pulmonaria* 'Blue Ensign', with plain dark leaves and the richest ultramarine flowers, provides a perfect setting for wandering swathes of *Galanthus* 'S. Arnott'.

SURPRISING CHINESE LYCORIS

by JAMES W. WADDICK

Over 10 years ago, I went to Hangzhou in eastern China as part of a study and collection trip focused on China's incredible native irises. After marveling at the iris specimens in the Herb Garden of the Hangzhou Botanical Garden (in China irises are considered medicinal herbs), I asked my guide, Mrs. Lin Jin-Zhen, to show me her favorite plants. She eagerly led me to another side of the garden.

That's were my jaw dropped: there, in a patch of seemingly bare ground perhaps 5' by 30', were a dozen labels in Chinese and Latin all naming different species and forms of lycoris. A couple of names were vaguely familiar, but most meant nothing. I knew just enough to realize that this bed of bulbs represented a treasure house of plants rarely seen outside of China. But because it was May, the plants were dormant.

After returning home, I corresponded with my newfound friends and was able to arrange to import some bulbs. It turns out that these Chinese species have rarely been introduced into U.S. gardens and have never been available to most gardeners. Now, after growing most of the species and more than 20 hybrids, I can recommend the best of these surprising plants. But first, some background.

The genus *Lycoris*, which belongs to the amaryllis family (Amaryllidaceae), consists of 23 or more species. Most are Chinese, some are Japanese and a smattering of others occurs from Korea to Burma and Vietnam. All species lose their foliage by May in my Kansas City garden (USDA Zones 5/6). They bloom in late summer to fall on bare stalks with no foliage and so should be marked carefully.

There are two major groups of lycoris. The first is represented by *L. squamigera*, a bright pink-flowered species that is a garden standby in the northern half of the United States. It goes by a lot of local names, some of them quite colorful, including naked ladies, naked boys and even pink flamingo flower. The most appropriate, however, is surprise lily. Plants in this group have regular flowers with smooth petals. In early spring they produce husky foliage that withers and goes dormant by May. In late summer, leafless stalks appear bearing large flowers. This group, which constitutes about half the total species, tends to be more northern in origin and thus hardier.

The red surprise lily, *L. radiata*, an old-time plant that is common throughout the South and bears bright scarlet flowers, represents the second group of species. These surprise lilies have

new lycoris hybrid

smaller flowers with narrower, twisted, spidery petals. Their foliage appears in late fall and stays evergreen all winter until it too withers and goes dormant by May. The bare flower stems rise a bit later — September in my garden. This group comprises the more southern and more tender species, although *L. radiata* is totally hardy here in western Missouri.

Oddly, both of these common species are sterile (seedless)

Lycoris squamigera in a garden setting

Lycoris sprengeri

Lycoris chinensis

species has proven bone hardy in my garden. In early spring it produces some husky but attractive foliage that is gone by mid-spring; later-emerging perennials such as hostas easily cover the bare ground. Because it is a fertile species it can be propagated by seed or allowed to self-sow.

Other hardy yellow-flowered species include *L. caldwellii*, with pale yellow to creamy white flowers of semispidery form, and *L. straminea*, whose straw-yellow petals are sprinkled all over with fine red spots, making it very distinctive within the genus. Both bloom late and have good-size, 3" flowers.

By far the most tender species is the yellow-flowered *L. aurea* (sometimes incorrectly identified as *L. africana*). It is often listed in catalogs, but the true species is rarely offered. *Lycoris aurea* has nearly 3'-long, very succulent leaves that are damaged by the slightest frost. It is suited only to Zones 9 and 10. Often confused in the trade is the mostly Japanese species *L. traubii*, which, although closely related to *L. aurea*, is somewhat hardier (to Zone 8) and has leaves to only 1' long.

triploids. They are extremely vigorous growers, however, and can be multiplied easily by digging and dividing the clumps of bulbs in June or July.

The New Varieties

Golden surprise lily (*L. chinensis*) is perhaps the most striking of the new lot. My patch of a dozen bulbs puts up 30" stalks in August and produces heads of 3" to 4" bright yellow-orange lilylike flowers when little else is blooming. The clump is visible from the street and has caused a few screeching brakes and exclamations of "What's that?" This

White surprise lily (*L. longituba*) is an all-white "version" of *L. squamigera*, being similar in size, growth, flower form and hardiness. The large, pure white trumpets are close enough to Easter lilies to confuse novices. If you can grow pink surprise lilies, you can and should grow *L. longituba*. This species also has an uncommon pale yellow form known as *L. longituba* var. *flava*. The trumpets of delicate yellow are a great addition to the palette of lycoris colors.

What I call the "electric" surprise lily (*L. sprengeri*) is a surprise indeed. The 3" flowers have clean, bright pink petals whose outer

Lycoris caldwellii

Lycoris radiata

seed. Why wasn't it introduced to horticulture years ago along with *L. squamigera*?

Lycoris haywardii might justifiably be called the dwarf pink surprise lily. At just over 1', it is the smallest of those described so far and has deep pink-violet flowers that appear in late summer before those of *L. squamigera*. Hybridization experiments suggest it is a natural sterile hybrid with *L. sprengeri* as one of its parents. The plant's small size and intensely colored flowers make it suitable for all kinds of garden sites.

These are only a few of the new species coming from China; at least a half-dozen others are also distinctive, desirable additions to the shade garden.

Many lycoris hybrids have been made both artificially and naturally. These run a gamut of dawn-to-dusk colors, from palest yellow, pastel tangerine, apricot and peach to deeper pink and bicolors. They also exhibit variation in size, vigor and hardiness, although most involve the northern species and have proven fully hardy for me.

Garden Use

The Chinese species seem especially suited to climates with continental weather patterns — hot dryish summers and cold winters. These condi-

tips can only be described as electric blue — a color that comes as a shock on first view. The plant has spring foliage (although in milder climates it may come up in fall) and is totally hardy. In bloom, the bare stalks reach about 15" in height in August and September. It amazes me that this gardenworthy plant has only rarely been seen outside of China. It is a perfect shade-garden stalwart, with every desirable characteristic: good size, hardiness, amazing flowers, modest foliage, freedom from pests and diseases and fertile

tions allow some degree of summer baking. In mild climates with cool summers and no periods of really hot weather (such as the British Isles) the bulbs apparently do not do as well.

They also tend to dislike being transplanted unless it is done at the proper time. When the plants are totally dormant, from about June to August, they can be dug, dried off and replanted without adverse effect. Unfortunately, this is not the usual time for commercial bulb sales. Lycoris bulbs held dry until the traditional

Lycoris radiata in a garden setting

Last August I visited Hunan Province in central China and saw several wild lycoris species in bloom. They were growing in deep shade and very moist-to-soggy soils near a small stream — definitely deep woodland conditions.

In cultivation, too, lycoris grow best in shaded woodland but tolerate a few hours of full sun each day. Adding organic matter to the soil is always a good practice, but the plants do well even in my heavy clay soil. They seem to have no preference regarding pH. Although they do not need supplemental summer watering, they will tolerate some moisture during their dormant period. They have no specific pest or disease problems.

Culture and Planting

The most important feature of these bulbs is that they bloom at a time of year when most other flowers in the garden have slowed down and little else can produce this kind of show. The new Chinese varieties bring a wide palette of colors to augment the other somewhat startling bright pink of the old-fashioned *L. squamigera*. Since they bloom on bare stems it is best to underplant them with neighbors that retain good foliage during bloom season. In my garden they are surrounded by hostas, epimediums and hellebores. All the various lycoris flower colors are very pleasing, mostly calming pastels that mix well. If you grow a range of species you can have flowers from late July right up to frost. As a final bonus, they make excellent cut flowers if they are cut when the first flowers open on the stalk and immediately plunged into water. They'll last longer indoors than they do outside, especially if you garden in an area subject to hot, drying late-summer winds.

The new lycoris are more than just surprise lilies — with their eye-catching colors, hardiness and welcome bloom period, they are "wow" lilies. Just be careful you don't plant these too close to busy traffic; otherwise, you might hear screeching brakes, too.

bulb-selling period (October, November or later) may simply freeze and die without settling in. Late planting may well be why some species such as *L. radiata* are considered tender in the North. Properly planted during their natural dormant period, they do fine. Find a supplier who sells dormant bulbs in summer or potted, growing bulbs to make sure they will settle right into your garden. Bulb sizes vary from 1" in diameter for *L. radiata* var. *pumila* to more than 4" for *L. longituba*. When calculating planting depth, use the old standby rule of two to two and a half times their height to the bottom of the bulb.

THE GREATER PLEASURES OF THE LESSER CELANDINES

by PAMELA J. HARPER

Ranunculus ficaria 'Flore Pleno'

When using popular names, gardeners don't all speak the same language. To some, "celandine" means *Chelidonium majus*, a plant in the poppy family, also called greater celandine.

This is a useful plant, and a pretty one, for naturalizing in shady, root-filled woods along with such other toughies as golden archangel (*Lamium galeobdolon*). Having had its fling in my garden, it has been ousted in favor of the showier and equally amenable *Stylophorum diphyllum*, or celandine poppy. This flourishes in a spot few perennials would tolerate, among the suckering stems of red chokeberry (*Aronia arbutifolia*). Seedlings extending this terrain, often unnoticed among the lush vegetation of summer, must be weeded out when the bright yellow flowers signal their presence in spring, for this winsome colonizer is an object lesson in the principles of compound interest paid at a generous rate: one, ten, a hundred, a thousand . . .

These both belong to the poppy family, but what I call celandine, *Ranunculus ficaria*, belongs with the buttercups. Some call this lesser celandine. Lesser! In size, yes; in numbers, no; in beauty and diversity, absolutely not. As a child, I ate first from my plate what I liked least, leaving the best for last. Adopting now the same approach with this little celandine, I'll dispose first of the distasteful part, then the rest can be relished.

The celandine, in its wild form, spreads very rapidly, both by seed and by proliferation of tiny tubers. If you can't stomach that, keep it off your garden plate. Once I saw it carpeting acres of daffodil fields, flowering along with the daffodils, bothering them not at all, being so much shorter — an enchanting sight if you can grant it an acre or so to play in.

I grow the wildling in a roadside ditch beyond the fence, while within my garden sundry selected forms hold me enthralled in the early months of the year. Most of these aren't unduly invasive, given a reasonably watchful eye. Not for the rock garden, perhaps,

Ranunculus ficaria 'Double Mud'

melt away, so quickly and neatly do they disappear. This pattern of late-winter bloom and early dormancy enables them to tolerate overplanting with herbaceous plants. I have them under Japanese painted ferns (*Athyrium niponicum* var. *pictum*) and hardy orchids (*Bletilla striata*). These increase less rapidly than others growing under shrubs in less crowded conditions.

My collection began with a single-flowered white form, a gift from Elizabeth Lawrence, my friend and mentor, when I was coming to grips with gardening in Virginia. Recently, I was able to return it to her garden's new owner. Elizabeth didn't know its name, but 'Randall's White' and 'Salmon's White' look nearly the same, particularly if you don't concern yourself with such minutiae as to whether or not petals are slate-flushed on the reverse.

'Primrose' and 'Citrina', with flowers that open lemon yellow and fade to cream, also resemble each other. One of these is tucked under a buttercup winter hazel (*Corylopsis pauciflora*) with flowers of matching yellow. The other is in front of an epimedium with flowers of complementary pale purple.

Next came *R. f.* 'Flore Pleno', widely disseminated in my area as marsh marigold. There's a superficial resemblance to the double-flowered marsh marigold (*Caltha palustris* 'Flore Pleno'), but no one familiar with the two could possibly confuse them. The celandine is more compact and smaller in all its parts, and the flowers are

but a joyful sight under and among shrubs, where control amounts to little more than removing seedlings that don't resemble their parent and aren't worth preserving in their own right. I don't find this a tiresome chore, but it could be reduced, perhaps eliminated, by growing only double-flowered forms, which seem less prone to self-seeding.

In my coastal Virginia garden, growth starts around the turn of the year, when rosettes of burnished leaves appear, prettily and variously patterned, snuggled flat and neat against the ground. Flowering begins as soon as the weather warms up, usually by late February, continuing for six weeks or more. Flower petals, typically bright yellow, are as highly polished as those of their buttercup relatives. *Ranunculus ficaria* subsp. *ficariiformis* is my first to flower, usually beginning sometime in February. This is the tallest form I grow, with the largest flowers and leaves.

When their flowering is done, celandines seem almost to

a clearer yellow. 'Flore Pleno' makes its way up through a mat of a dusky purple periwinkle (*Vinca minor* 'Atropurpurea'), a captivating combination that leaves no bare ground when the celandine goes dormant.

There have been no seedlings from 'Flore Pleno', or from another double, the neat and compact 'Collarette', which has leaves reminiscent of cyclamen in shape and patterning and flowers as precisely crafted as the cogs in a watch, with stubby petals evenly spaced around a green-eyed hub. Its warm, orange-yellow color harmonizes nicely with tufts of the dwarf golden sweet flag (*Acorus gramineus* 'Minimus Aureus'). A short row of 'Collarette' edging a mulch path leaves no obvious gap when it goes dormant; the path just looks a bit wider at this point.

Single-flowered *R. f.* 'Cupreus', with light orange petals shading into copper at the base, grows around and among *Epimedium ×warleyense*, which is shorn in late winter of its wiry-stemmed leaves, by then shabby, to better display its flame-colored flowers rising over those of the celandine. This epimedium is a thinly wandering grower; most grow too dense for underplanting. Fresh new epimedium leaves later fill the space left vacant by the celandine.

Ranunculus ficaria 'Brazen Hussy', found and named by Christopher Lloyd, is such a knockout few can resist it. Even wary rock gardeners have been known to risk it among their tiny treasures. Its scintillating buttercup-yellow flowers are set against light-reflective leaves of dark chocolate brown which stand out against brown earth but are much better displayed against golden gravel, gray stone or the chartreuse foliage of *Lysimachia nummularia* 'Aurea'.

When I was growing up in England, "coppernob" was a term used for those

Ranunculus ficaria 'Coppernob' tucks neatly under *Acorus gramineus* 'Ogon'

with auburn hair, affectionately by adults, often tauntingly by children. The celandine named *R. f.* 'Coppernob' also attracts a great deal of attention. A child of 'Brazen Hussy' and 'Cupreus', it combines dark foliage with coppery orange flowers that fade to banana yellow and finally to white. I have it in front of a showy evergold sedge (*Acorus gramineus* 'Ogon').

Man and nature continue to experiment, and there's been quite a rush of new celandines. I haven't yet found a double white to rival the double bloodroot (*Sanguinaria canadensis*) that blooms at the same time, but if the flowers of one I christened 'Ivory Buttons' before I knew that its proper name was 'Double Mud' (also acquired

as 'Double Cream') are neither as large nor as snowy white as those of the bloodroot, they are also not as evanescent. I once left for a trip when its flowers were newly opened to find that they were still there to greet me after three weeks away. Their flattened pom-poms of gentle, poised appeal have petals of ivory flushed with slate. 'Green Petal', by contrast, is a clown, raising a smile from those who find pleasure in the quaint and curious. Its conglomeration of green and yellow paddle-shaped petals form a scrambled, semidouble flower that looks as if its been stirred with a fork.

Whatever next? I have starts of several others and eagerly await the first sight of their flowers. Celandines are addictive.

TREASURED TRILLIUMS

by CAROL BISHOP MILLER

The trillium is the most diverse and yet distinctive of the spring-blooming ephemerals that grace our native woodlands.

It is notable enough — and various enough — to have attracted some splendid common names: toadshade (for its fancied resemblance to a toad-size umbrella), wake-robin (for its appearance with the fine robins) and birthroot (for its medicinal uses associated with childbirth).

The origin of the name trillium explains itself, for the parts of a trillium flower and accompanying leaves occur in threes or multiples of three. Thus a typical mature stem is capped by a whorl of three leaves (technically bracts), while the solitary flower, which may last two weeks or more, sports three petals, three sepals and six stamens.

The fruit is a triple-chambered berry with many seeds. In many trillium species the seed is dispersed by ants, which feast on the *elaisomes,* or fatty bodies, attached to the outside of the seed.

Every trillium is either sessile — with its flower perched directly atop its whorl of leaves — or pedicellate, with the flower raised on a short stalk, or pedicel. While some 50 species inhabit temperate North American and Asia, the hotbed of diversity lies in the southeastern United States, where roughly half reside. Here in the rocky, wooded hillsides of northern Alabama where I live, the most abundant is *Trillium cuneatum* (USDA Zones 5–7), labeled whippoorwill flower in books (though I've never heard anyone call it that). A succulently handsome plant, *T. cuneatum* bears outstretched oval leaves, conspicuously mottled in shades of dark and pale green, atop a stout 4" to 18" stem. The petals, which can be up to 4" long, are held uptight, perpendicular to the usually purple-tinged sepals, and are normally brown or maroon, though occasionally greenish or even yellow. The scent, when detectable, is faintly unpleasant, for, like many sessile trilliums, *T. cuneatum* is pollinated by carrion flies.

As with most trilliums grown in the garden, *T. cuneatum* is accommodating as to soil as long as it is humus-laden and moist (but not soggy), and requires at least light shade, either deciduous or evergreen. Trilliums perish in full sun, while in utter gloom they may fail to bloom at all.

A similar species with even more striking foliage is Underwood's trillium (*T. underwoodii;* Zones 5–7) native to the southern coastal plain, though reported hardy as far north as Michigan. The silvery midveins of the 8" leaves are flanked by splotches of three or more deeply contrasting shades of green. The stem is very short, so that the tips of the umbrellalike leaves brush the ground. The maroon or brownish flower is anticlimactic by comparison.

The South's most distinctive sessile trillium is the twisted

Trillium erectum

Trillium grandiflorum

trillium (*T. stamineum;* Zones 5–8) confined in the wild to a narrow band stretching from west Central Tennessee through eastern Mississippi and the western half of Alabama almost to the Gulf Coast. The stocky stem, 12" to 18" tall, bears wide softly mottled leaves capped by a spidery, sessile bloom with outspread purple petals that are curlicued like the propellers of an airplane. The anthers and sometimes the purple-tinged sepals may curl as well. A yellow-flowering form has been reported.

Perhaps the most garden-worthy sessile trillium is the yellow-flowering *T. luteum* (Zones 5–7) of the southeastern hill country. Bearing a strong resemblance to *T. cuneatum*, it is crowned by a bright yellow, 1.5" to 3" wide blossom, which glows like a flame in the shaded garden. This trillium is readily distinguished from yellow forms of other sessile trilliums by its delightful lemony fragrance.

No doubt the trillium most familiar to the gardening public is the large-flowered trillium (*T. grandiflorum;* Zones 3–9), whose 2"- to 4"-wide nectar-bearing flowers stretch regally above the broadly handsome, unmottled leaves atop 3" pedicels. Opening white, then gradually aging to pink, the overlapping petals with their undulating edges flare outward from the golden anthers. With a natural range that covers the eastern third of North America, *T. grandiflorum* is perhaps the least fussy trillium to grow. Double forms and forms with green-striped petals sometimes occur.

Often confused with *T. grandiflorum* is the best trillium (*T. flexipes;* Zones 4–7), which also bears large white blossoms well above a parasol of apple-green, diamond-shaped leaves. The blossoms of *T. flexipes,* however, have a more leathery texture than those of *T. grandiflorum* and feature cream colored anthers. With a range that sweeps across two-thirds of Cana-

culture & NOTES

Trilliums are readily swapped among gardeners north, south, east and west. Though fall is best, they can be moved any time of year as long as they are protected from damage and dehydration. Depending on size, dormant rhizomes should be planted 2" to 4" deep. Provide the transplant with humusy, moist well-drained soil and protection from strong sun and drying winds. Top with a fresh layer of leaves or other organic mulch every autumn to keep the soil rich and moisture retentive.

Though the foliage may die away when summer's heat and drought arrive, the buds that produce the following year's leaves and flowers are formed on the rhizome in late summer. Thus plants of considerably greater size and vigor result when ample water is supplied all summer long. Grow trilliums among other moisture-loving shade plants like coleus, impatiens, false Solomon's seal and ferns to make sure that the rhizomes receive summer moisture.

Trilliums are extremely long-lived plants, but they do occasionally meet with adversity. Slugs and deer find the leaves tasty. Rodents relish the rhizomes. Armadillos and other grub-seekers unearth the rhizomes as they paw through the mulch. Viral or fugal diseases have been reported to affect trilliums, although rarely.

Trilliums do not increase rapidly. Only a few offsets are formed on the rhizome each year, and, depending on species and conditions, a trillium seed may take four to nine years to yield a plant large enough to bloom.

Trillium seeds have a double dormancy. Unless planted immediately upon maturity, before the seed coat hardens, a seed will not germinate until the following spring, when it will send forth only a radicle, or primary root. The spring after that, a single small leaf, the cotyledon, will appear. It may be another year or two before the full complement of three leaves appears atop the stem, and a year or two beyond that before we see the first flower.

da and funnels down to northern Alabama, this sweetly fragrant trillium, like *T. grandiflorum* forms vast colonies under suitable conditions.

The best trillium must be distinguished from the nodding trillium (*T. cernuum*; Zones 3–9), whose somewhat smaller, purple-anthered, white to pinkish blossoms dip beneath the leaves on down turned pedicels. Thus the flower stares at the ground, while he swept-back leaves gaze upward. This trillium, in turn, is easily confused with Catesby's trillium (*T. catesbyi*; Zones 5–8; 8"–14"), whose down-facing golden anthered, white flower (resembling an angel in flight beneath the winglike leaves) slowly ages to pink. Both of these bashful bloomers appeal primarily to enthusiasts who are willing to savor their charms down low and up close.

Far more pizzazz is to be had with the painted trillium (*T. undulatum*; Zones 3–9), whose prominently white or pale pink blossom is dabbed with a central halo of crimson. Rare this far south, painted trillium needs constantly wet, cool, very acid soil, preferably on the sandy side, with lots of mucky humus mixed in. Indeed, it is one of the few trilliums that is truly at home in a bog, and it will bloom even in black shade. Everything about the painted trillium, including its scarlet fruit, is showy.

Purple trillium (*T. erectum*; Zones 3–9) is another attention grabber. Sometimes called stinking Benjamin, or wet-dog trillium, this husky 2' boasts a striking 2.5"-wide flower the color of dried blood which exudes an aroma likened to that of a rain-soaked mutt.

Trillium rhizomes reportedly contain steroids, and *T. erectum*, a conspicuous species which ranges from eastern Canada to the Deep South, has been used in folk medicine possibly more than any other for everything from hastening childbirth to treating snakebite and asthma.

Purple trillium is easy to grow except in heavy, poorly drained soils. It combines especially well in the shade garden with *T. grandiflorum*, which matches its height and relishes the same conditions. Gardeners will be interested to know that there are also yellow and white forms of *T. erectum*.

The closely related Vasey's trillium (*T. vaseyi*; Zones 5–7) is larger still, and the 4"-wide blossoms, which dive beneath the leaves like those of the nodding trillium, have a faintly pleasant scent.

The East, of course, has no monopoly on garden-worthy trilliums. The western states' answer to *T. grandiflorum* is the white–flowering, pedicellate *T. ovatum* (Zones 5–9), which grows to 20" and is available in many forms and several named cultivars, including the double-flowering 'Edith'. The flower of *T. ovatum* usually (but not always) turns pink or even red with age.

The West's *T. chloropetalum* (Zones 6–9) and *T. kurabayashii* (Zones 6–8) are ses-sile trilliums that strongly resemble the *T. cuneatum* of Alabama. *Trillium petiolatum* (Zones 4–6), from the mountainous Northwest, equals our *T. stamineum* in novelty. While short of stem, its curious round leaves are el-

test-tube TRILLIUMS

Researchers are laboring to find ways to increase trilliums more rapidly and inexpensively and lessen the strain on existing natural populations. Some nursery growers have long practiced rhizome-scoring. They dig up the rhizome shortly after bloom and make a shallow cut around it near the newest growth. Bulblets form around the cut. The following year the rhizome is dug up again and the bulblets removed and planted out.

At the Mount Cuba Center for the Study of Piedmont Flora in Greenville, Delaware, Director Dick Lighty and his colleagues are experimenting with selected clones of *T. grandiflorum* that naturally form large clumps quickly. The group is also exploring techniques for raising trilliums from seed with the lowest possible labor input.

Even in tissue culture, trilliums grow more slowly than many other plants, according to Dr. Valerie Pence, head of the Plant Conservation Division of the Center for Reproduction of Endangered Wildlife (CREW) at the Cincinnati Zoo and Botanical Garden. Through test-tube cloning, CREW has created a colony of *T. persistens* (Zones 5-7), a dangerously rare species. Dr. Pence points out that cloning is desirable for horticultural purposes, but not ideal when a goal is reintroduction of a species to a wild area because clones lack genetic diversity. And even a test-tube trillium needs perhaps five more years of growth to bloom.

Commercial propagation of trilliums continues to be a slow and difficult undertaking. While we wait for a practical means for making it cheaper and simpler, let's enjoy most trilliums in the wild rather than in the garden.

The trillium's greatest modern enemy is man. We replace its habitat with malls and highways. We introduce Asian honeysuckles and other exotic competitors that overrun the woodland floor, especially where logging or fire opens the tree canopy. And we dig and sell the rhizomes, sending off thousands every year.

Visit a natural health products store and note the jars of dried wildflowers, including trillium rhizomes, lining the shelves. We gardeners are no more innocent. In our unbridled acquisitiveness, we are in large part responsible for endangering the survival of many trillium species.

Some nurseries advertise their stock as "nursery-grown" when it is in fact nothing of the kind. The rhizomes have been poached from private property or, increasingly, from state or national parks. Then, so severely weakened by dehydration or tough handling that they are near death, they are stuck into pots and grown until sold.

We must only deal with sources that can prove to our satisfaction that they offer only nursery-propagated material. (I find the best approach is to talk with any potential supplier.) Admittedly, such totally legitimate enterprises are few and far between. To date, it is much more profitable to sell trilliums collected from the wild than to propagate them over a period of several years by seed or division.

evated far above the sessile blooms on exaggerated petioles, or leaf stems, an arrangement that gives the plant a look of stark surprise.

Big, succulent trilliums add richness to the spring shade garden, but rock gardeners wax eloquent about the charms of more diminutive species. The dwarf white snow trillium (*T. nivale;* Zones 4–6) is a dainty delight that pushes through the snow with the snowdrops and the early crocuses and unfurls its saucy white pediceled blossoms weeks before its cumbersome cousins poke their noses above ground. Native from western Pennsylvania to Nebraska, dwarf snow trillium is fond of limy soil and is best tucked into its own pocket among rocks. It is easily snuffed out by pushy neighbors and even by mulch that is too deep.

Trillium rivale (Zones 6–9; to 10"), from the Oregon-California border region, rivals *T. nivale* for daintiness. The flower is unusual in that it may open flushed with pink, then fade to white, and may be freckled with crimson.

Trillium Kurabayashii

CARDIOCRINUM, KING OF THE LILIES

by CHARLES O. CRESSON

> For years, I dismissed the notion of growing the spectacular giant lily *Cardiocrinum*
> *giganteum*, assuming that it was suited only to the cool, moist climates of Britain
> and the Pacific Northwest.

Yet in spite of the hot, steamy Philadelphia summers my garden endures (USDA Zone 6), I have managed to grow this gem of the Himalayas with relative ease. During the past 12 years it has flowered four times. One might attribute my success to microclimate, but perhaps, given its geographical range, cardiocrinum possesses greater adaptability than it is credited with. Whatever the reason for my success, this giant lily is worth a try among adventurous gardeners.

A True Lily — Almost

Cardiocrinum giganteum is closely related to the true lilies and was once classified as *Lilium giganteum*. Indeed, the name cardiocrinum means "heart lily" in Greek. Yet important differences, most notably the wide, heart-shaped leaves with branched veins, have prompted taxonomists to separate it and two or three other species into their own genus.

Cardiocrinum plants are slow to mature, requiring at least four years to reach flowering size. During their juvenility, their wide, hostalike leaves grow up to 2.5' long. The year the plant flowers, it pushes up a stem which may reach 12' in height and hold 20 or more flowers along the top 20". The lowest buds open first, beginning a two-week bloom sequence during the climax of which nearly all flowers are open. The narrow, funnel-shaped flowers are greenish white on the outside with a purplish-maroon stain within. The light lily scent of daylight hours intensifies in the evening and permeates the air with a strong fragrance that I find reminiscent of jasmine spiced with clove. In Britain and the Himalayas, cardiocrinum flowers July through August. In the United States, bloom time ranges from mid-June to August, depending on the coolness of the climate.

Bulbous, 3"-long seed capsules ripen in autumn, splitting into toothed segments that spread somewhat like the petals of a tulip. The thousands of paper-thin seeds, tightly stacked within, are then spread by the wind like confetti. With its toothed pods, the dry stalk is a spectacle in itself, both in the autumn garden and in the corner of a room as a decorative reminder of a gardener's proudest moment. The novelty of this botanical curiosity is ample justification for its reprieve from the compost heap.

raising more CARDIOCRINUMS

Sowing paper-thin giant lily seeds is an act requiring great faith and patience, but it is much less expensive than buying bulbs. Moreover, the range of adaptibility among numerous seedlings increases the chance of success in your garden. The seeds need two periods of stratification under cold, moist conditions, with a warm, moist period between. In late summer to early winter, I fill plastic 4" pots within ¼" of the top with commercial soilless potting mix. I then spread the seed evenly over the surface and cover it with fine gravel. The gravel holds the seed and the soil in place during watering and helps maintain the soil's moisture, but will not cake and inhibit germination. I put the pots in my 35°F to 40°F attic, where there is minimal light, protection from mice and I can check them regularly. If germination occurs during late winter, I move the pots to a cool, frost-free windowsill until spring. In summer, the pots reside in my screened porch, where temperatures range from 70°F to 90°F and the seedlings are protected from animals. When the seedlings have become dormant, I return them to the attic for the winter before planting them outside the following spring.

While cardiocrinums are monocarpic and die after flowering, the small bulblets that form around the base of the stem can be separated and replanted while the plant is dormant to preserve a clone or to hasten propagation. Depending on size, these bulbs will flower in three to five years.

Secrets to Success

Unlike most other lilies, cardiocrinum bulbs are composed of relatively few bulb scales and do not form stem roots above the bulb. They need to be planted shallowly, so that the top of each bulb is even with the surface of the soil. Covering the bulbs with a mulch such as leaf litter (I use oak leaves and pine needles) is essential to keep the roots cool. Once they have become established and begin to gain size, cardiocrinum bulbs resent disturbance and, once established, will become stunted if moved. For this reason, purchase and plant only young bulbs.

Cardiocrinums require loose, uniformly moist, well-drained soil. Standing moisture will rot the bulbs. Since they are heavy feeders, amending the soil with abundant compost will help produce tall stems. I have had good results by spreading 3" to 4" of good compost and leaf mold over a bed of well-drained soil and mixing it in to a spade's depth, about 12". I then provide supplemental feeding, preferably with a slow-release organic fertilizer, early each spring.

At first, I grew the giant lily only in a deep, loose soil that was laden with leaf mold. Successive generations of offsets have provided enough plants to experiment with different locations and conditions in my garden. I risked one in a much heavier and shallower clay soil with slower drainage that I amended with leaf mold. With a leafy mulch, it did just as well and seemed to appreciate the moister conditions. The one uncompromising requirement of the giant lily is that it must be planted in a shady location. A single day in direct sunlight will scorch the leaves to an absolute crisp. With filtered shade and good root protection, however, my giant lilies have survived temperatures in the 90s with ease.

Giant lilies are nearly pest-free. My biggest problem has been with baby slugs, which love to eat holes in the leaves. (At least they have small appetites.) I've found it easy to control slugs by collecting them at night with a flashlight. Aphids may feed on the flower buds in May and June, but are easily controlled then with a single application of insecticidal soap.

Showing It Off

The choice of a planting site for cardiocrinums in your garden will, of course, be dictated by where it will grow, but if possible, aim for a location with dramatic potential. A good place would be where the plants can be viewed from a distance, such as rising up from among low herbaceous perennials, or where they can be perched on a slope. Planting cardiocrinum bulbs in large groups not only improves their effect, but creates a stand where bulbs of all ages can provide blooming plants every year. Avoid crowding them behind taller plants where the juvenile specimens will not receive enough light. Neither should the bulbs be placed in the front of the border — the foliage won't be attractive in late summer, if it remains standing at all. A woodland groundcover such as *Phlox stolonifera* will help compensate for the disappearance of foliage. In my garden, *Primula kisoana* fills this function, forming a colony in the mulch under my giant lilies that bears pink flowers as the lily leaves unfurl in April. Alas, its foliage does not persist in late summer either. For a background to the giant lily, I grow the woody companion plants *Rhododendron arborescens*, *Hydrangea anomala* subsp. *petiolaris* (climbing hydrangea) and *H. heteromalla* (a rare white Chinese lace-cap hydrangea), all of which bloom at the same time in my garden.

Hot and Cold

In warm climates, such as mine, you will probably find that the giant lilies tend to die down in midsummer, although mature plants continue to stand as their seeds ripen. If this happens, don't be alarmed — it is a normal occurrence. Cardiocrinums in warmer areas seem to go through their growth cycle faster, blooming earlier and escaping the heat with a siesta. If the bulbs are kept cool with a mulch, you can expect them to remain firm the following spring.

Despite their tender reputation, cardiocrinums should be winter hardy in parts of the Northeast where they can revel in the cooler summers. I have never lost a plant over the winter here in Zone 6 and I read that they have been successfully grown in Rochester, New York, as well as Ohio, Massachusetts and Rhode Island and as far north as Vermont. The winter protection that cardiocrinums receive in their native habitat from a blanket of snow can be easily emulated with mulch. Emerging leaves may also need protection from late frosts, given by covering them with a box or blanket for a night or two.

No plant speaks more compellingly of the far corners of the world than the regal giant lily of the Himalayas. Yet this sentinel of the forest is within the reach of many North American gardeners. Why not share the adventure?

IVY-LEAVED CYCLAMEN

by PAMELA J. HARPER

Why, when asked to recommend plants for dry shade (a question that comes up at every large gathering), have I never thought to mention the ivy-leaved cyclamen (*C. hederifolium*)?

I reel off the standard cast of sturdy groundcovers — ivy, lamiastrum, pachysandra, periwinkle, *Symphytum grandiflorum* and, if all else fails, mulch on which to stand containers of impatiens. This cyclamen, as tough as it is charming, beats them all. It puts up with heat, considerable cold (it is hardy to USDA Zone 5), deep shade and shallow soil. In summer it is dormant and untroubled by drought. I've grown it for 40 years and never known it to be anything but healthy and good-looking. You need patience (or a lot of money) to achieve a large stand, but then it is yours for life. It has thus far even escaped (touch wood) that scourge of my present garden, the vole. Are the tubers not tasty, or are they perhaps poisonous? Or is the cyclamen spared because it grows near the surface and voles tunnel lower down? It is, anyway, a decided blessing to count. Another boon is that rabbits don't seem to find the foliage palatable.

The pink or white flowers appear in autumn. The leaves that follow and carpet the ground through winter are lovelier and more varied than any others I know, most of them exquisitely patterned in silver and green. Occasionally one with leaves of plain green or nearly solid silver will appear. The size and shape of the leaf also varies. You cannot count on all the seedlings to resemble their parent, but you can be sure there will be no ugly ducklings.

growing cyclamen FROM SEED

During my early gardening years I happened, by luck or instinct, upon an easy way of raising cyclamen from seed. Take a lightproof lidded container, such as those that hold soft margarine, make a few drainage holes in the bottom, fill to within 1" of the top with a commercial peat-based compost, space the seeds .25" apart, cover lightly with horticultural vermiculite, put on the lids and stand the containers (which can be stacked) where they won't be overlooked — the kitchen windowsill, for instance. Ignore them for the first month, then check once a week to see if the seeds have germinated. If only a few have started to grow, put the lid back on – the seed germinates best in the dark and those already growing will come to no harm for a few weeks. When about half have germinated, replace the lids with clear plastic held in place by rubber bands. After the last frost date, mine go into a shaded frame, those that haven't germinated still in their lidded containers, the others uncovered. Here they stay for another year, watered when necessary, the frames covered in winter. If you don't have a frame, or won't be there to keep an eye on them, plant them out — they'll survive if undisturbed.

What will *C. hederifolium* not put up with? Soggy soil, certainly, and the tubers may not survive being planted upside down, which has probably happened often with unpotted tubers, whose bottom is smooth and rounded with no vestige of roots, which come mainly from the sides. (Nursery-grown tubers are shipped in pots, making it easy to tell which side goes up.) When the tubers are planted as they should be — shallowly — birds and squirrels sometimes toss them out of the ground when searching for food or burying acorns. Pegging down black plastic netting prevents this. Invisible under a thin layer of mulch, the netting is permanent. Chicken wire can be used but will eventually rust away.

The ideal site for cyclamen is under large shrubs or deep-rooting deciduous trees with leaves of moderate size — oaks, for instance, where there's summer shade, some winter sun, and an annual mulch of fallen leaves. If the leaves are blown, or you insist on tidying them away, compensate with a light top-dressing of leaf mold, sandy or loamy soil, compost or finely ground bark. Where heavy rain leaches nutrients from the soil, a scattering of a general fertilizer every couple of years will do no harm but it isn't essential, so err on the side of too little rather than too much.

Happy cyclamen self-sow in abundance. When the flower fades the stalk coils down like a spring and the round seedpod develops close to the ground, opening to deposit the seed on top of the mother tuber, where the strong seedlings will crowd out the weak unless you intervene. A patch can be extended much more rapidly if little bunches of seedlings are held between finger and thumb and gently wiggled to extract the tiny pearly tubers, which should be replanted 1" or 2" apart to give them more room to grow. Do this at flowering time, before the leaves grow thick enough to hide the seedlings. They will flower within two years.

chapter four
STEP-BY-STEP PROJECTS
for shade gardeners

layering a RHODODENDRON

by Oliver E. Allen

Some plants multiply themselves by putting down roots from pendulous branches that touch the ground. The forsythia is one of the most notorious examples — it roots so readily it can become invasive if left untended. The phenomenon is known as layering, and it can be used as a remarkably simple way to propagate plants — especially woody ones — for which neither seeds nor cuttings are satisfactory methods. An elegant rhododendron that you'd like to duplicate would be a prime candidate. What you do, in effect, is bury a section of a branch in the ground. If you follow certain precautions roots form, and before long you can cut the new plant loose to exist on its own.

The botanical key to the process is a cut that you make in the branch before burying it. The wound interrupts the flow of nutrients, causing the sugars to accumulate, and this seems to promote the formation of roots. The parent plant supplies some nourishment to its offspring until you separate the two and is in no way harmed by the exercise.

Although several kinds of layering are practiced (such as air layering, in which the wound is enclosed in sphagnum moss and wrapped with plastic but then is not buried) so called-ground layering is the simplest. The job is best begun in the early spring when the ground can be worked but before a new growth has started. To layer a rhododendron you will want to select a healthy, young shoot low enough on the plant to be bent to the ground; the older and woodier the branch, the less likely it is to root. To be sure of results, try layering two or three shoots (so long as you can find young, low ones predisposed to layering). The only supplies you need are root-promoting powder (available in any garden center), a forked twig or short length of heavy wire, some peat moss (or compost or leaf mold) and sand or perlite, and a sharp knife.

1 prepare the soil

Because roots form best in a light, porous medium, you should loosen the soil in the area where the branch will be buried. Cultivate the soil; break up any lumps; add a good heap of peat moss, compost or leaf mold, plus some sand or perlite; and mix thoroughly. Remove enough of the resulting mix to leave a shallow hole 3" deep.

2 make a careful cut

Using your knife, make a cut about halfway through the branch on its underside, preferably near a node or branching point and 6" to 8" from the end. Do not flinch; a common mistake is to make the cut too shallow to induce root growth. Wedge a sliver of wood (a wooden match stick serves nicely) into the cut to keep it open, and dust the newly bared wood with rooting powder.

3 secure the branch

Lay the branch into the hole with the cut at the lowest point (facing downward) and the end pointing up and out the other side. Anchor the branch using your forked twig or heavy wire (bent like a staple); otherwise the wind will soon dislodge the whole affair. Once the branch is securely pinned you may want to insert some soil behind the part leading out of the hole to point it more sharply upward, thus giving the resulting plant a straighter stem; but be careful not to bend it so much as to break it. Some gardeners loosely attach the tip of the branch to a stake to guide it vertically. Fill the hole with soil mix and tamp down well with your feet.

4 keep it moist!

Except for one paramount concern, you need pay no attention to the layered branch for at least a year. The concern — and it is vital — is that the soil around the buried section remain moist. Dryness can swiftly kill young rootlets, and if the ground is dry for even a day as the roots are forming, the new plant may be lost. The solution is to keep a good mulch in place over the layered area (black plastic is a particularly efficient moisture-conserver) and to keep an eye on weather conditions during the warm months. During any rainless spell pull back the mulch every other day or so and feel the soil. If it is on the dry side, give it a good but gentle soaking and replace the plastic.

5 check for new roots

For reasons no one really understands, the amount of time needed for new roots to develop varies widely among genera. Rhododendrons root very slowly, and it is likely to take at least a year, and more likely two, for roots to grow. The trick is in determining when roots have become sufficiently established and when to sever the plant. Since the shoot can put on new top growth without putting down roots, you cannot reply on that measure. One way to check is to lift the staple and gently tug on the shoot. If it offers resistance, roots have formed. Do not expose the rooting area to the air for long or it will dry out. When the roots are well established, sever the supporting branch near the soil line (and then cut the resulting branch stub back to the nearest node or to another branch for appearance's sake). The young plant is best left in place for a month or two after it has been severed to ensure that its roots are well established. At that point it can be transplanted.

growing BLOODROOT FROM SEED

by HEATHER MCCARGO

1 *scout some plants*

The first step is to find a healthy blood-root population by looking for the plants when they are in bloom in the early spring. Make sure you have correctly identified the plant, and check with your state's Natural Heritage Program to make sure that bloodroot is not listed as an en-dangered or protected species. If the plants are not growing on your land, you'll need to obtain permission from the landowner before collecting.

raising bloodroot

Bloodroot (*Sanguinaria canadensis*) is a harbinger of spring in deciduous woodlands of eastern North America. In March or April, when the permanent thaw finally arrives, bloodroot sends up its dainty, short-lived flowers, which have white petals radiating from yellow centers. As the flowers fade, large, deeply lobed, rounded leaves emerge. With adequate precipitation they will remain in good condition into the fall.

Like many spring-blooming wildflowers, bloodroot has a reputation for being diffi-cult to propagate. This is due to a lack of understanding of its life cycle. Bloodroot, like many other wild species, can easily be grown from seed; the trick is having access to fresh seed, which must be sown immediately upon ripening and waiting for it to germinate the following spring.

2 *harvest some seeds*

Bloodroot seeds begin to ripen about six weeks after blooming, which can be at any time from mid-April to early June, depending on where you live. Bloodroot seedpods are green, 1" to 2" long and shaped like little kayaks. As the pods ripen they begin to yellow and eventually split down one side to reveal shiny brown seeds with fleshy white attachments called elaiosomes. The seeds begin to fall out immediately and are carried off by ants, which eat the fatty elaiosomes and discard the seed, thereby planting it. Be watchful, or you will miss the seeds. Once one seedpod has ripened and split you can collect other unopened pods on nearby plants, so long as the seeds it contains are brown.

3 *sowing the seeds*

Seeds must not be allowed to dry out, or they may never germinate. Sow the seed in a flat or pot at least 2" deep, or directly in a prepared bed in the shade. If possible, use a compost-based seed-starting medium mixed with coarse builder's sand in a ratio of two parts soil medium to one part sand. Cover the seed with a layer of sand as deep as the seeds are wide. Water immediately, pushing down any seeds that show through the surface. Then place the seed flats in a shady location and cover them with a spun-bonded row cover, such as Reemay.

why SEED?

Growing wildflowers from seed has many benefits. Rarely is it ethical to dig wild plants and move them to your garden. Healthy populations of wild plants, however, will produce an abundance of seed. Collecting a small percentage of it will give you plenty of potential seedlings, usually without adversely affecting wild plant populations. Additionally, when you grow wildflowers from seed, you are helping to preserve genetic diversity within that species, which helps a species adapt to changing environmental conditions such as cold, heat, drought, excessive moisture or even pollution. This genetic diversity is the raw material of the process of evolution. Vegetatively propagated plants (from cuttings, root divisions, and tissue culture) are genetically identical to the parent plant and thus lack this potential to evolve over time.

4 wait for germination

Bloodroot is not a domesticated plant, and like all wild plants, its seeds have evolved to germinate when conditions enable them to grow most successfully. In the case of bloodroot, this means that the first juvenile leaves won't appear until the following spring and you will see nothing in your flat or bed all summer, fall and winter. Your job, therefore, is to make sure the seed flats do not dry out, become overtaken with weeds (which the shade and the Reemay will reduce) or used as a litter box by the cat. This is not difficult; it just takes patience and commitment.

5 care for the seedlings

Seeds will germinate in the early spring, sending up little round, lobed leaves. Once the seeds germinate, young plants need to be fertilized every couple of weeks with a mild liquid fertilizer, such as diluted liquid seaweed. At the end of the first growing season, in September or October, transplant seedlings into bigger pots, with several seedlings per pot, or directly in the garden.

more seeds

Other wildflowers that can be grown from fresh seed include baneberry (*Actaea* spp.), bluebeard lily (*Clintonia* spp.), celandine poppy (*Stylophorum diphyllum*), liverleaf (*Hepatica* spp.), marsh marigold (*Caltha palustris*), twinleaf (*Jeffersonia diphylla*) and Virginia bluebells (*Mertensia virginica*).

The following wildflowers will germinate after the second winter: bellwort (*Uvularia grandiflora*), false Solomon's seal (*Smilacina racemosa*), Solomon's seal (*Polygonatum* spp.) and trillium (*Trillium* spp.).

dividing a
FERN
by BARBARA JOE HOSHIZAKI

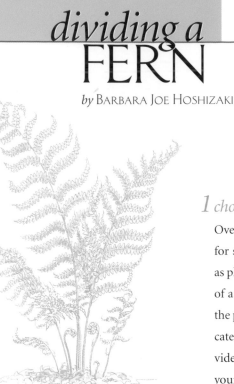

1 *choose a suitable offshoot*

Overgrown ferns are a good source of divisions. Examine the fern for secondary growing points or offshoots. These are identifiable as places where new fronds are emerging (or will emerge) at the tip of a stem (rhizome). The connection between these offshoots and the parent plant may be above or below ground. Once you have located more than one offshoot, you will know the fern can be divided. Remember, though, that even if they have several offshoots, young ferns are often too small to produce vigorous divisions.

2 *prepare a nursery bed*

Before you begin dividing your fern, you will need to have a location prepared to receive the divisions. Most ferns like shade or partial shade and grow more luxuriously in protected sites away from drying and battering winds. Loose, humus-rich soil is preferred. Turn the soil to break up clumps and incorporate peat moss or leaf mold if it is not sufficiently friable. Additions of perlite or coarse sand will improve drainage and help prevent overwatering.

ferns by division

Ferns are like other foliage plants in that they can impart a sense of repose and serenity to a landscape. In their method of reproduction, however, ferns are quite unlike other plants. Ferns do not reproduce by seed, but rather by spores and a two-stage growth cycle that is referred to as "alternation of generations." When you want to increase the number of ferns in your landscape, you can propagate ferns from spores, but it is much simpler to increase your ferns vegetatively by digging up a mature specimen and dividing it.

Ferns can be divided in both spring and summer, although the earlier you divide the plant, the longer the division has to recover. Candidates for division are ferns that form clumps or have stems that branch above or below ground. A few of these include wood ferns (*Dryopteris* spp.) and ostrich fern (*Matteuccia struthiopteris*), which produce offshoots that can be separated from the main stem, and lace fern (*Microlepia strigosa*), which is a subtropical species that forms clumps with many growing points. The East Indian polypody (*Microsorum grossum*) is a common tropical fern that can also be divided. Ferns with only one growing point, like most tree fern species and some Polystichum species, cannot be divided, however.

3 make your cuts

Dig up the entire plant that you are going to divide, using care to keep the roots intact. You will need a sharp, serrated knife, such as a bread knife, to make the divisions. A typical division consists of a portion of rhizome with one or more growing points and its attached roots and leaves. Although healthy roots or leaves are not absolutely necessary, fern divisions establish themselves much more quickly if they are present. Large divisions give the best results, and the more growing points in each division the better. For small ferns, the rhizome length in a division should be at least 2". For larger ferns, 4" or more will do. Cut only the stem and avoid cutting the roots. Gently pull the pieces apart so the attached roots remain intact.

4 proper planting

Using a sharp knife, trim away dead or broken stems, fronds and roots. Be especially careful not to bruise or break the growing point. To avoid prolonged root exposure, plant the division in its new site as soon as possible. Make the hole deep enough so the growing point will be level with the soil surface. Do not plant the division too deep or the growing point may rot. Spread the roots out in the hole and replace the soil. Gently firm the soil in place. Replant the parent fern in the same way.

5 aftercare

Immediately after planting, water the fern thoroughly. Use a watering can with a fine sprinkler head to prevent washing away the soil. If the plant topples, straighten it up and support it with a rock or stake. If the day is hot or windy, cover the division with a tent of newspaper or other material to prevent it from drying out. Keep the area around the new division moist but never soaking wet. The fronds may wilt at first, and they can be trimmed off if they do not recover in a few days. The emergence of new fronds indicates successful establishment of the division. Apply a weak solution of fertilizer to hasten growth at this stage.

training a
FUCHSIA STANDARD

by Sonny Garcia

Whether a garden is formal or informal, a well-placed standard can dramatically enhance its beauty. One of the most versatile plants for this garden art form is the fuchsia, with its broad range of flower shapes, sizes and colors, and often striking foliage. Other suitable options include shrubby plants such as artemisia, bay, myrtle, rosemary and santolina.

To make a 36" standard, choose a fuchsia with large course leaves and big flowers, such as 'Hidcote Beauty' or 'Voodoo'. For an 18" or smaller standard, select a variety that is finely textured and has small flowers. Fuchsia 'Little Gem', 'Isis' and 'Oriental Lace' are all good candidates. Just be sure to give the plant some shade during the hottest part of the day.

1 *select a suitable plant*

Although it is possible to start a standard from cuttings, it is quicker to visit your local nursery and pick a plant that is already growing. This plant should be upright in habit, with a strong, straight leader. While you are there, choose an appropriate container. Heavy terracotta pots with a hole for drainage are always the best, whether the standard in intended for display by itself or will be blended into the border. A 12" pot is suitable for a 36" standard, while a 6" one is fine for an 18" specimen. Repot the plant using a standard potting mix with some water-absorbing polymers and a few granules of time-release fertilizer.

2 plant your cutting

Use a sharp, sterile knife or scissors to remove all side branches from the plant. This will encourage top growth. Do not remove leaves growing directly on the trunk. To support your standard, insert a redwood stake or plastic-coated metal rod close to the trunk and push it all the way down to the bottom of the pot. (You will need a 2' stake for a 36" standard; a 1' stake for an 18" one.) Use raffia or twine to gently tie the trunk to the stake at four evenly spaced intervals.

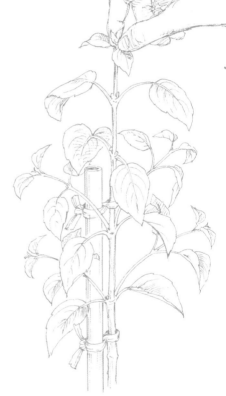

3 pinch for bushiness

Once the plant has three sets of leaves above the top of the stake, pinch back the growing tip. This will cause the side shoots to grow and form a bushy head. Pinching will also increase the number of buds produced. Do the same to the side shoots when they have a minimum of three sets of leaves. As soon as the head has reached a pleasing size (one that is in proportion to the trunk and pot), stop pinching so blooming may begin. Gently remove any leaves that remain on the trunk, or allow them to drop off naturally.

4 aftercare

To thrive, fuchsias need regular watering — in fact, it is almost impossible to overwater one if the pot has good drainage. Frequent misting will keep the foliage clean and help control pests. For continuous bloom, apply half-strength doses of a complete liquid fertilizer every two weeks. Remove old and faded flowers often. Since fuchsias blossom on new wood, you should cut back the head of your standard by one-third each fall. (This will also keep the plant the appropriate size and shape.) If you live in a cold-winter area, bring your plant into the greenhouse or a well-lit room before the first frost.

pruning a LARGE TREE LIMB

by OLIVER E. ALLEN

The best time to remove a limb from a tree is winter, except in the cases of maples, birches, and other trees that produce copious sap. For such trees, summer is a better time (in subtropical climates, the end of the dry season is preferred). If you can easily reach the limb with a ladder, there is no reason not to tackle the job yourself. However, if you're thinking about climbing up into the branches to remove a limb, don't. This is a dangerous task best left to professionals who have the proper training and equipment.

You can ensure your own safety by following a few precautions. Be certain your ladder rests on a firm base; if the ground is soft, set the ladder on some planks. Lash taller ladders to the tree and have someone hold the base of the ladder while you work. But keep other spectators away. And note where the limb will fall, making sure its drop won't injure people or plants. If its fall might damage a valued shrub or shade-loving groundcover that is finally established, tie a rope around it, pass the rope over another limb higher in the tree, and lower the cut limb slowly to the ground.

1 the case for cutting

There are many reasons why you may need to remove a sizable limb from one of your trees. The limb may be damaged, diseased, or dead. It may be shading the area below too much, and you are setting out to let in more light and air. Or it may just displease you; the tree would look better, you decide, without that particular branch.

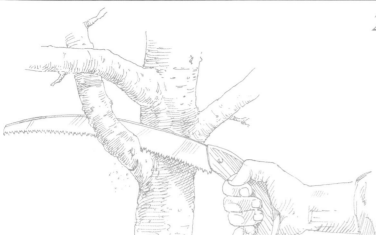

2 *choose the right tools*

Any limb with a diameter greater than one inch should be sawed. For limbs up to two inches in diameter or slightly larger, and for limbs growing close to another, a narrow, curved pruning saw is the ideal tool and is easy to use, as it cuts by a pulling rather than pushing action. For cutting larger limbs, a straight pruning saw with teeth on both sides of the blade can be used. But handier for most amateurs (because it can be used for jobs other than pruning) is a bow saw, which has a detachable blade mounted on a C-shaped frame. In any case, do not use a chain saw, which is far too perilous for someone balancing on a ladder.

3 *make the first cut away from the trunk*

Make your first cut on the underside of the branch one foot out from the trunk, cutting upwards until the branch begins to bind the saw blade. This upward cut will prevent the limb from tearing away the trunk's bark as the limb begins to fall. The second cut is then made from the upper side of the limb, an inch or so farther out. Cut straight down until the branch breaks off, which it will do as you approach the lower cut.

4 *make the final cut close*

Finish the job by removing the stub that remains. With larger branches you may want to make two cuts again. In any event, make your cut close to the trunk – just beyond the branch collar – and perpendicular to the direction the branch was growing. This ensures a small a wound as possible. If you can hang your hat on the stub that remains, it needs further trimming. However, do not cut into the branch collar. The collar provides a chemical barrier to prevent decay, and cutting into that area makes the tree vulnerable to infection.

ASIATICA
P.O. Box 270
Lewisberry, PA 17339
717-938-8677
www.asiaticanursery.com
Online catalog

BLUESTONE PERENNIALS
7211 Middle Ridge Road
Madison, OH 44057-3096
800-852-5243
www.bluestoneperennials.com
Free catalog

BUSSE GARDENS
17160 245th Avenue
Big Lake, MN 55309
800-544-3192
www.bussegardens.com
Catalog $3

COLLECTOR'S NURSERY
16804 NE 102nd Avenue
Battle Ground, WA 98604
360-574-3832
www.collectorsnursery.com
Online catalog

THE CROWNSVILLE NURSERY
P.O. Box 797
Crownsville, MD 21032
410-849-3143
www.crownsvillenursery.com
Free catalog

EASTERN PLANT SPECIALTIES
P.O. Box 5692
Clark, NJ 07066-5692
732-382-2508
www.easternplant.com
Catalog $4

FAIRWEATHER GARDENS
P.O. Box 330
Greenwich, NJ 08323-0330
856-451-6261
www.fairweathergardens.com
Catalog $4 for two years

FANCY FRONDS NURSERY
P.O. Box 1090
Gold Bar, WA 98251-1090
360-793-1472
www.fancyfronds.com
Online catalog

FORESTFARM
990 Tetherow Road
Williams, OR 97544-9599
541-846-7269
www.forestfarm.com
Free catalog

FRASER'S THIMBLE FARMS
175 Arbutus Road
Salt Spring Island, BC
Canada V8K 1A3
250-537-5788
www.thimblefarms.com
Online catalog

GARDEN VISION
63 Williamsville Road
Hubbardston, MA 01452
978-928-4808
E-mail: darrellpro@earthlink.net

GIRARD NURSERIES
P.O. Box 428
Geneva, OH 44041-0428
440-466-2881
www.girardnurseries.com
Online catalog

GOSSLER FARMS NURSERY
1200 Weaver Road
Springfield, OR 97478
541-746-3922
www.gosslerfarms.com
Online catalog

GREER GARDENS
1280 Goodpasture Island Road
Eugene, OR 97401-1794
800-548-0111
www.greergardens.com
Free catalog

KLEHM'S SONG SPARROW PERENNIAL FARM
13101 East Rye Road
Avalon, WI 53505
800-553-3715
www.songsparrow.com
Free catalog

MARY'S PLANT FARM
2410 Lanes's Mill Road
Hamilton, OH 45013
513-894-0022
www.marysplantfarm.com
Catalog $1

MOSS ACRES
Rd 3 – Box 3170
Honesdale, PA 18431
866-438-6677
www.mossacres.com
Online catalog

PINE RIDGE GARDENS
P.O. Box 200
London, AR 72847
479-293-4359
www.pineridgegardens.com
Catalog $5 for 6 issues

PLANT DELIGHTS NURSERY

9241 Sauls Road

Raleigh, NC 27603

919-772-4794

www.plantdelights.com

Online catalog

RARE FIND NURSERY

957 Patterson Road

Jackson, NJ 08527

732-833-0613

www.rarefindnursery.com

Online catalog

ROSLYN NURSERY

211 Burrs Lane

Dix Hills, NY 11746

631-643-9347

www.roslynnursery.com

Catalog $3

SAVORY'S GARDENS

5300 Whiting Avenue

Edina, MN 55439

952-941-8755

www.savorysgardens.com

Online catalog

SENECA HILL PERENNIALS

3712 Co. Rte. 57

Oswego, NY 13126

www.senecahill.com

Catalog $4 for two years

SISKIYOU RARE PLANT NURSERY

2825 Cummings Road

Medford, OR 97501

541-772-6846

www.srpn.net

Catalog $3

SUNLIGHT GARDENS

174 Golden Lane

Andersonville, TN 37705

800-272-7396

www.sunlightgardens.com

Free catalog

TRIPPLE BROOK FARM

37 Middle Road

Southampton, MA 01073

413-527-4626

www.tripplebrookfarm.com

Free catalog

UNDERWOOD SHADE NURSERY

P.O. Box 1386

North Attleboro, MA 02763-0386

508-222-2164

www.underwoodshadenursery.com

Online catalog

THE VARIEGATED FOLIAGE NURSERY

245 Westford Road

Eastford, CT 06242

860-974-1077

www.variegatedfoliage.com

Online catalog

WE-DU NURSERIES

2055 Polly Spout Road

Marion, NC 28752

828-738-8300

www.we-du.com

Online catalog

WOODLANDERS

1128 Colleton Avenue

Aiken, SC 29801

803-648-7522

www.woodlanders.net

Catalog $4

index